# Keep the Wheels Down

**1973 to 1997**
**Val Mohr**

Thank you for helping the Slattery

Val Mohr

# Publication Data

First Printing    March 2012    Staples, Yuma, USA
Second Printing  April 2013    Create Space, Charleston, USA
Third Printing    March 2015    Create Space, Charleston, USA
Fourth Printing  August 2016  Priority Printing, Edmonton, Canada
Period of time    1973 to 1997  (Football 2015)
Fourth Printing Edited by  Irene Gaudet, Success Publications, Creativity Corner Inc.
Cover Picture    Edmonton River Valley
Author    Val Mohr Fort Sask., Alberta, Canada
Copyright    Val Mohr
Truck related pictures by Val Mohr

Football related pictures  Post Media Copyright; **Material republished with the express permission of Postmedia Network Inc.**
Edmonton Sun Photographers: David Bloom, Ian Kueerak, Codie McLachlin, Tom Braid
Calgary Sun Photographer:  Al Charest
Winnipeg Sun Photographers:  Chris Procaylo, Kevin King
Spruce Grove Examiner Photograpgher: Mitch Goldenberg

Book Profits Donated to Stollery Children's Hospital Foundation Edmonton. Alberta Canada

Authors contact  valmohr@aol.com

ISBN-13:    978-1-896737-65-2

# Information:

A portion of all Book sales will be donated to the Edmonton Stollery Children's Hospital. **Reason for This**: When our second grandson was born He required heart surgery prior to leaving the Hospital. **Outcome**: Today he is married and working in the Engineering Field and has a son, our first great-grandson Nash Nicholas Mohr. **Follow Up**: Perhaps each small donation made will bring help to some child and hope to the parents and grandparents who must bear the pressure of watching a sick child fighting for survival.

The first book was not edited, however the sick children at the Stollery Children's Hospital do not care they were happy that you made a donation by purchasing a book. Total donation at time of printing is over $11,000.00 These Children and the Author thank you for your support.

*Val Mohr*

## Special Recognition

It goes beyond saying that the Doctors, Nurses and all other employees should receive special recognition for the many hours devoted to the children of the Stollery Children's Hospital. With out their sincere dedication the Hospital would not be known as the best Children's Hospital West of Toronto. The hospital has some 220,000 visits per year. The hospital admits the sickest of the sick children of Western Canada. Just to name a few were Macy Denham of Camrose born at twenty-four weeks is now doing well. Four year old Cheyanne Mattern of Calgary had a double lung and heart transplant at the same time. She is now riding her bike and going to school. Dillian Reid of Lloydminster was born not breathing; after four major surgeries plus twenty-five minor surgeries plus over two thousand hospital procedures during his six hundred thirty-four days at the Stollery, he is now doing well. Edmonton can be proud of their two major sports teams, The Edmonton Oilers and the Edmonton Eskimos who spend many hours visiting the children in hospital. I am pleased to have received permission from Post Media Licensing to include some pictures of the 2015 Grey Cup Champion Edmonton Eskimos. I do hope you enjoy the pictures as well as the rest of the book. All of the profits of the book go to the Stollery Children's Hospital Foundation. I want to thank each person in eight provinces fourteen states as well as four other countries that have received books. To date over eighteen thousand dollars ($18,000) has been donated since the first book was published. All donations that I receive are passed directly on to the Stollery Children's Hospital Foundation.

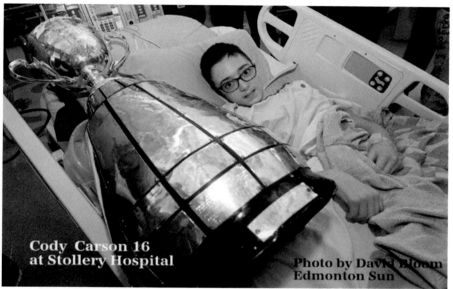

Cody Carson 16
at Stollery Hospital

Photo by David Bloom
Edmonton Sun

Material republished with the express permission of Postmedia Network Inc.

*Thank you Edmonton Eskimos for a job well done in 2015.*

*Val Mohr*

# Dedication

This book is dedicated to the two women in my life who believed in me and gave me the support and dedication that I so much needed and depended on.

My first wife June who supported me when I wanted to leave a secure job after twenty years and go after a dream. The care I received during my accident was above and beyond.

My wife Bernice who gave me the help, love, and encouragement to continue on after the fire, the bank troubles, and the passing of my son Darrell. If it had not been for her our success would not have been possible. I am so happy to share my retirement with you Bernice.

# Prologue

This book is written as a lasting history of VLR Carriers Ltd. The start to the end of a period of time in Transportation History of Alberta. It contains some interesting experiences of the men and women who worked hard to keep the oil industry in Alberta moving. If it was not for men driving trucks on roads in adverse conditions as mentioned within our Province we would not be enjoying the standard of living we have today.

*Val A Mohr*

# About the Author

I, Val Mohr was born in Edmonton and grew up on a small mixed farm outside the village of Josephburg about eight miles east of Fort Saskatchewan. I attended a two room country school from grades one to eleven. The school closed one room and became a one room school for grades one to eight. I finished grade eight in Josephburg and then my parents moved to Fort Saskatchewan where I went to High School. I continued post secondary school at Vermilion and graduated from the Vermilion School of Agriculture in 1956.

I started the work force in May of 1956 at Peace River Glass Company as an operator. In September of 1956 I switched and started at Sherritt Gordon Mines Limited. Here I worked in the Lab for four years.

In 1958 I accepted an invitation to attend a nursing graduation on a blind date. Things turned out and in 1960 I married June Read who had graduated from nursing in 1958. Darrell was born in 1962 and Rhonda was born in 1965.

In 1964 I transferred from the lab to the Traffic department. In 1973 we started VLR Carriers Ltd. In 1975 I left Sherritt with just under 20 years with the Company.

In 1976 I had my traffic accident which put me in hospital for 3 months. In 1980 my wife June passed away with cancer. In 1981 I married Bernice. We put together the "Brady Bunch," six teenagers between 14 and 18, three boys and three girls. In 1991-1992 I was president of the Alberta Trucking Association. In 1994 Darrell passed away with cancer. In 1997 we sold VLR Carriers Ltd.

On December 31, 1997 I retired from active Working. Since my retirement I have travelled the world visiting close to seventy countries. Watch for my next book, "Tips – Trips and Tours".

# Introduction

Story-telling and preserving history is an art that the author has tried to pass on in this his first book, "Keep the Wheels Down".

How deals were made and problems solved are well worth reading about in this book. Val Mohr tells about the hardships when they first entered the trucking industry hauling product related to the Black Gold Industry of Alberta. As we travel the modern Highways of Alberta today, we do not think of the problems our drivers of Yesterday had to face to overcome the many hardships that today we take for granted.

## Magazine write ups

The fall 2013 issue of the Western Canada Highway News had a full two page write up on Keep the Wheels Down book on Page 26 and 27

The Fort Record had a half page article in their October 3, 2013 paper on the book Keep the Wheel Down. The Fort Record writes a second article in their August 21, 2014 indicating $8,000 donated to the Stollery Children's Hospital Foundation

The winter 2015 addition of the Heroes Magazine put out by

the Stollery Hospital Foundation had an article about Val Mohr and his book Keep the Wheels Down. The article says more than $10,000 has been donated to the Stollery Foundation.

# Accidents

To have written a book and not go into what I have learned over my years in the trucking industry both as an owner of a trucking company and my affiliation with both the Alberta Trucking Association and Canadian Trucking Association, as to some of the reasons for trucking accidents and not share my views would be a total mistake to the trucking industry and to the general public. As you read the book and look at the pictures, you may get the feeling that we were a very careless trucking company and had no respect for safety. This cannot be further from the truth and I would like to go into some of the facts about our company and to some points applying to trucking in general.

When we started our trucking company VLR Carriers Ltd. the first thing that I did was make sure the first two lease operators had a good driving record. Our first two lease operators, Noel Berube and Dave Thomas, had clean driving abstracts and had no records of ever having being involved in any driving mishaps prior to coming to work for VLR Carriers Ltd. They were both family men that put safety at the top of their priority list. I felt that good drivers should be rewarded for jobs well done and as a result when a driver reached 300,000 accident free miles they were rewarded with some kind of reward that would show what they had accomplished. Both Noel and Dave reached the magic 300,000 mile plateau and as a result the company gave them each an expense paid trip for two to Disneyland. This was accomplished in just over three years of driving. As time went on other drivers received the following: trips for two to Victoria (was common), a fly in fishing trip to a fishing lodge in Northern Alberta, and numerous salmon fishing trips to Terrace, B.C. The salmon fishing trips were the most popular as there were four men that travelled by motor home and stayed in hotels upon their arrival. A fishing charter was used to provide for the best fishing. Everyone returned with salmon.

It is not easy to travel for over three years and not have some type of accident as many of the roads were not highways. If a driver did everything possible to avoid an accident and an occurrence still occurred, the driver often may be forgiven and the occurrence would not go against his driving record. Let me give you two examples. The first case the driver loaded at a plant site located on a new company lease road that had not as yet been gravelled. Our driver put chains on all his wheels including the steering axle as well as the trailer and he still slid off the road. He was not held to blame as he had done everything possible to prevent the accident. When a driver chains up it is referred as having jewelry on all his wheels.

The second major accident that we had was similar in that the driver had chained up all his wheels and was chained behind a D8 cat to get pulled out, even with all the wheels chained up the trailer as well as the tractor slid off the road and upset in the bush below. We were lucky that the oil company paid for all the repairs as it was their cat that was towing us at the time of the accident. An accident like this we would never hold the driver to blame. The accident in both of the above cases the driver's record would show accident no fault of drivers.

I would like to list some of the reasons that I have found causes accidents in the trucking industry. Many of these same reasons can be used for general highway accidents.

1.     Drivers with not enough experience for what they are driving. Drivers hauling     loads without proper training on the type of the load.

2.     Drivers driving too fast for the condition of the roads. It is not road conditions that causes accidents but instead it is failing to drive to the road conditions that causes accidents.

3.     Drivers using drugs or alcohol when having control of a vehicle. Over the life of VLR Carriers we were involved in three fatality accidents. In all three accidents the driver of the other vehicle was under the influence of alcohol. In one case over three times the limit.

4.     Drivers driving too many hours and could be tired. All our drivers had to use tack cards which kept track of hours driven. We made sure our drivers stayed in the required legal driving hours.

5.     A common mistake is a driver drives off the road and tries to make a correction to get back on the road and rolls the unit. We tried at all our safety meetings to have the driver keep the unit on its wheels and drive directly into the ditch. Taking the unit into the ditch on its wheels is much cheaper to remove than to have to set it up on its wheels. Safety meetings were held about every two months.

6.     Drivers being distracted by using a phone, CB or trying to change a CD on their radio.

7.     Drivers trying to show off to other drivers while driving.

8.     Drivers trying to pore coffee or eat while driving.

9.     Drivers driving when windows are dirty. Keep them Clean.

10.     Drivers using drugs to keep awake. DO NOT USE!

11.     Drivers having to make sudden turns to avoid

something on the road.

12.    Drivers making sudden turns to avoid animals on the road. We always told our drivers it is better to hit a dog, deer or even a moose than to make a sudden turn which usually involves in an upset.

We had found that by driving a little slower, a truck gives the rest of the traffic more time to pass. Reducing the speed a truck is travelling by only 5 to 10 km/h is made up in fuel saved. It is amazing how much fuel is saved by simply driving a bit slower. We found rewarding drivers for safe driving does not cost but saves the company considerably. We would give all the drivers a special gift when they as a team reached a million miles accident free. We would post monthly how they were making out. It was interesting how as the team of drivers they would start policing each other as they got close to the magic million miles. At the time of selling we would reach a million miles in just over five months. At the time the company was sold we had one driver with close to 3 million accident free miles, about three drivers over a million miles, and the balance of our drivers all over 250,000 accident free miles. We had a group of drivers that we were proud of.

# Contents

# How it all began 1973

The telephone rang as I was sitting at my desk in my office at Sherritt breaking the silence of the early morning. "Good morning Val this is Larry Laird."

"Hi Larry what gives me the surprise of this call?"

Larry and I had gone to High School together in Fort Saskatchewan. Larry's parents moved to the Fort from Innisfail to build houses. My parents moved to town from Josephburg just out of the Fort. Larry was one or two grades ahead of me, but we knew each other.

We were both now working for Sherritt Gordon Mines Ltd. I was in the traffic department in charge of shipping all products that Sherritt produced world-wide. It was while I was working in the traffic Department that I got to know the cargo sales representative from Air Canada, Canadian Pacific and Lufthansa German Airlines. Sherritt was a new company in Western Canada and I was shipping all over the world for them by Air Freight.

One day the Lufthansa representative offered me a free air ticket to Edinburgh, Scotland. They were starting a new service from Canada to Scotland. When I mentioned it to my boss Mike Garvey he said I couldn't go and that he would go. I was heart broken but he promised me that the next trip I could go. "I said you remember that."

The following year I received a letter from the President of Lufthansa offering me a free ticket from New York to Frankfurt, Germany on their maiden flight with their new

1

747. I told Mike and he said "A deal is a deal" and soon I was off.

The following year Canadian Pacific offered me two free tickets to Mexico City and back. We took June's mother and the three of us went. I just took some holidays and simply did not say anything to anyone. I had learned how to handle this situation.

Larry had been in sample preparation and then moved to fertilizer Marketing. Larry had the gift of selling, He could sell a fridge to an Eskimo and then tell him he should have a deep freeze too. Larry had gone in partnership with Roger Henry who had started a fertilizer dealership on his farm selling Sherritt fertilizer. They had recently build a fertilizer outlet on the corner of highways 37 and 2. They were now thinking about selling anhydrous ammonia. It's a fertilizer containing 82% Nitrogen. It is transported and stored as a liquid but is applied as a gas. It must be handled with great care.

"Well Val the reason I'm calling is our company Sturgeon Valley Fertilizers as you know is thinking about getting into the anhydrous business. Roger and I were thinking that perhaps we should own a trailer to haul the product. We were wondering that if we purchased a trailer that you with your connections maybe able to keep it busy during the off season. Mainly in the winter months."

"Well Larry let me think about it and I'll get back to you."

It was a day or two after that that I called Larry back with my answer.

"Hi Larry, about what you had called me about I had given it some thought. My answer is I am prepared to help out under one condition."

"What's that Val?"

"It's simple if I help you out I want part of the action."

"Well Val that seems like a somewhat reasonable request. Why don't the three of us get together and discuss it?"

"Good idea. I suggest you and Roger come over to our place on the farm say next Friday evening and we will talk about it. Oh by the way bring your wives as I am sure June would like to meet them. The coffee pot will be on."

"Sounds like a date."

Friday night came and so did Larry and Pat and Roger and Marilyn to our farm. Larry knew where we lived as he had purchased hay from us for cattle he had with our neighbour. I had not met Pat and Marilyn prior and the only one June knew was Larry. The women went into the living room and talked about the usual things that women talk about. The three men sat around the kitchen table and decided what had to be done.

It was decided that the first thing we had to do was form a company and put the trailer in the name of the company. We now required a lawyer. Roger said he knew a lawyer who was a friend of his. "Good" you can make contact with him and have him do up the necessary paper work. Roger then contacted his friend a Mr George Brosseau who then became our company lawyer. At the meeting we had to have a name so we decided to use the first three letters of each of our names. VLR Carriers Ltd was chosen for Val, Larry and Roger.

George gave the names to his secretary to fill in on the papers. Wendy only knew Roger so he became President. Larry became Treasurer and the only women partner named Val became the Secretary. Did Wendy ever look when the three of us walked in to sign the papers! We all had a good laugh over it. I never ever let Wendy forget it.

When we decided to form the company we knew we would have to each put some money in to make it fly. Our plan was to invest as little as possible and no way was it to take any bread off our own tables. Upon checking we found we could have a trailer built in Texas for approximately $30,000. Since Sturgeon Valley Fertilizers used the CIBC (Canadian Imperial Bank of Commerce) that was who we should deal with. Larry knew the manager and set up an appointment to meet with him. Larry and I met with the Manager, a Mr. Hank Robothern, to explain what we wanted and what we required from the bank. Hank said they would loan us the money and we had to put up 25%. We said okay and it was agreed the bank would loan us the money. We would open an account and deposit money into it. We then decided that if each of us deposited $4,000.00 to our account it should keep us going till we received some cash flow. It was decided that I would run the company as I would have a better handle on things.

Our trailer was nearing completion in Lubbock, Texas and we soon would require someone to go get it. Working in the traffic department of Sherritt I got to know many truckers that were hauling in and out of the plant. I made arrangements with a Mr Paul Dupras who had a little shop in

4

Edmonton and had numerous trucks working for him. Some of the trucks were his which he was making payments on and hiring drivers for and others were lease operators. The one thing that I liked about his operation that if he gave us a truck and driver we could use the same driver all the time and not have to change drivers.

I was slowly starting to put feelers out and getting to know people who may know others that may at some time require tankers. We had not even hauled our first load when I realized we had a problem. The problem was that if we obtained some business for our trailer on a regular basis and something should happen to our trailer - WHAT DO WE DO? I immediately called a meeting to explain our problem to the partners. It was unanimous that we should order a second trailer.

Since Sherritt was just getting into the anhydrous business and would be requiring trailers. It would be part of my job to help locate trailers. It seemed a fit to purchase the trailer. We had one small problem that being we didn't have the money. Off to the bank again to have a meeting with our banker. I went there with a positive feeling not knowing what to expect. The meeting went positive at the start he listened to my sales spiel. He said. "Yes, we will give you the money. You have to come up with your one quarter as you have no collateral."
The same deal as the first trailer.

I said use the first trailer as collateral. I was informed it doesn't work that way as they already have a lien on that trailer. To make a long story short I simply told him I wasn't leaving until we had a deal without us putting in any extra cash. I finally convinced him to give us the extra money and we would pay a slightly higher interest rate on it. I insisted that it be a separate loan and not married to the first loan. Both loans were set up as a minimum payment over time based on a six month payment. This would allow us two make two payments a year after each anhydrous season.

Knowing what Sherritt was paying to haul anhydrous, I had it figured out how many loads we would have to haul to make our payments. Any extra hauling would be a benefit. This took a lot of long hand figuring ahead. This was in 1974 and we did not have a computer to do the numbers on.

We ordered the second trailer and it would be ready at about the same time as the first trailer. We sent two drivers down to pick up the trailers. I always felt a good image was important so we hired a girl to paint our name on both sides and the back of the trailers. They looked impressive and we were so proud. The trailers each received a number. The first was 174 and 274. The first number was the trailer number and next number was the year purchased. I later changed the number system with the first two numbers being the year purchased and the next number being the trailer number. They then became units 741 and 742.

Our first anhydrous season was very busy and payments were made on the loans much faster then expected. We paid down the second loan first as it had the higher interest rate. Working in the traffic department I was starting to meet other people in traffic positions. A traffic club was formed in Edmonton which was made up of all traffic people from Northern Alberta. It was called the Northern Alberta Transportation Club – NATC. It was just a social club which met once a month. They had golf tournaments and curling bonspiels. I got elected as treasurer of the NATC and had the job for two years. This gave me a good chance to get to know many people in the Transportation industry. The members came from manufacturing industry and the rail, air and the trucking industry in and around the Edmonton area. I was Sherritt's member.

Southern Alberta had an organization called the CITL standing for Canadian Industrial League. It was a working organization and soon a similar branch was established in Edmonton. Sherritt became a member and I attended regular meetings. It was through this association that I started to meet people from the oil and gas industry from Calgary. It was at one of these meetings that I met a person from Cigas who gave me our first job hauling NGL (natural gas Liquids). This was from a little plant at Peers Alberta to Gibsons unloading terminal on17th street.

**1975**

**Noel loading our first load of NGL Mix from Norcen plant at Peers, Alta.**

This became our backbone for our NGL hauling business.

7

The plant had storage for about three loads and we hauled about a load every second day when it was running good. This product was very clean similar to propane.

I called a meeting of the partners to advise them we no longer had a spare trailer as one trailer was now dedicated to full time use. If the trailer was to go down suddenly we could not use the trailers used for anhydrous as they would have to be steamed out first. A decision was made to buy another trailer, rush. Through my memberships in the various associations I knew of a person in Calgary that had a used trailer for sale. We called him and purchased it from him sight unseen. We took his word. It was an older trailer and heavier but it gave us the back up we required. It was referred to as the Richardson trailer and became unit 743. We purchased it from Richardson Trucking. It was cheaper then the first two we purchased from the USA and we didn't go to the bank for money. In fact, I never told the bank we had it. This trailer was the only trailer we had with a corkan pump. All of our other ones had blackmer pumps. The bank would have wanted to put a lien on it too. It didn't take me very long to not trust banks.

Things were going pretty good and soon we had the opportunity to bid on hauling propane to the coal mines at Coal Valley and Greg River in the Hinton area for Cigas. We got the business and things really took off. Rates were based on one way hauling however we were able to back haul from Peers so that really changed the economics when this happened. We treated our lease operators well on this movement and we did real good. Economy Carriers had the bulk of the business in Alberta but people were getting to know us.

Our business had started in 1974 and we already had three trailers. The anhydrous business was growing and so was our LPG business. After we started hauling for Cigas I got a call for a rate to haul a load of propane to Great Canadian Oil Sands (GCOS) camp at Fort McMurray. GCOS was the first camp that started in Fort McMurray.

We had a lease operator named Henry who was a very good trucker. He did, however, have a bit of a short fuse. Henry got to the plant site gate and the guard asked him for his union card. No one had told us it was a union site. The guard informed Henry he would have to get out and someone would drive his truck in and unload the trailer. Henry told the guard that unless they make his truck payments they can go to hell. I get paid to come up here and I get paid to go back and with that he went in around the gate house and back down the highway to Edmonton. He didn't get very far before lights were flashing behind him. He stopped and the fellow came over to the truck and said it is 36 below here and we need the propane for the bunk houses and the cook shack. Come and unload your load. He never had any more problems to haul up there after that first trip. Whenever Henry arrived they just waved and in he went. When someone else had to haul up there we had to have a union card. We were a non-union operation however we had a driver who at one time had a Teamster card. He would leave his card in the office and whoever went up there took the card. No one ever asked to see if the drivers name was the same as the union card. We hauled for years and never had a problem.

From time to time I would go in and talk to the bank manager about how things were going. This one time I was in the bank and was going to talk to Hank but was informed by his assistant that Hank was on holidays. She wanted to know if she could help. I said well yes I think so. I was wondering when the bank was going to take me out for supper. She said good idea when would you like to go? I said any time but just to keep it on the level I think our partners should also go. No problem I'll pick the spot and let you know. She picked a nice place in Edmonton and the four of us met for supper. As the night went on and the more wine she drank the more she talked. She said, "Do you know what it says in your file?" I said no. "It says on the cover, HANDLE WITH KID GLOVES."

Whenever Larry called me from his office or I called him we had to have a code in case someone came into our offices. We decided to use the word "Time". Whoever had the visitor would mention time in a sentence and the other knew that we had to hang up. We had to do this as there is always someone who is jealous or thinks you shouldn't be doing this on Sherritt time. This system always worked.

I had started at Sherritt in Sept of 1956 and had been in the traffic department for a number of years when my boss Mike Garvey who was perhaps one of the best traffic men in Canada was promoted to the Toronto head office. Our department was then put under new management. Our new boss knew nothing about transportation and as a result we often did not see eye to eye. It was at this time I had to make a decision to stay at Sherritt and put up with the lack of confidence of my boss or leave. I had talked to management about my problem but got no help or encouragement. June and I discussed it to some length and she said I would have to make that decision. VLR Carriers was growing and it was getting harder to keep from being noticed. I was a few months short of twenty years with Sherritt when I decided to shut it down with them. I did have faith that VLR would be a success so I handed in my resignation.

It was at this time that Paul Dupras offered me a job running his office and helping grow. Paul's wife Vivian worked in the office. Vivian and I got along well together and we enjoyed working together. Then one day she confided in me that Paul was having an affair. Shortly after Paul advised me that Vivian would no longer be working in the office. I was not surprised but he said not to worry as he had hired someone else. Your right it was his bosom sweetheart. We got along but only because I felt we should.

We now had four trailers and two were kept busy. The two lease operators that we had were originally from Paul. I had hired them to work directly for VLR Carriers. Their names were Noel Berube and Dave Thomas. They were both excellent employees and drivers. I could depend on them to look after the trailers. Paul had rented a vacant yard on the Manning Freeway to store his trailers and our tanks. He then moved in an Atco trailer. He set up an office for me and I was moved out to the trailer. I had my own telephone but could also answer his office calls. VLR did have a private line for their calls. I had an answering system on it. If we required minor trailer or tire repairs it was done in Paul's shop. I knew what was going on at the main office as the drivers both mine and his would drop in and keep me posted. I had only worked in the Atco trailer a short time when Paul came over to tell me my job would be finished on Friday. I could see it coming as things were not going to good for Paul.

Things, however, were going pretty good for VLR. Our accountants suggested to avoid paying a lot of taxes we

11

should each lease a vehicle. I had taken a new GMC pickup fully loaded. Roger and Larry each took cars. I had a canopy on it with all the extras on my pick up. It was what I was driving on my last day of work in Edmonton for Paul.


## Val's Accident

I was heading into Edmonton when a car stopped to let me go by at the junction of Hwy 15 and 37. There were no lights there back in 1976. A car went to pass the stopped car on the shoulder and hit black ice and came across the highway in front of the stopped car and I broad sided it at 60 MPH. I had my seat belt on. It was only a lap belt but it saved my life. I hit the car so hard that my engine came under the front seat. My right knee when through the dash as I reached for the brake. My face hit the steering wheel and broke it. The frame bent in the middle and the canopy split in the middle. The truck was a total write off. The other car was also a write off. The other driver lived but did lose one eye and was banged up pretty good. I unfastened my seat belt and got out and fell to the pavement. That was the last I remembered till I was in the hospital in the Fort Saskatchewan.

The doctors checked me over and decided to send me to the Royal Alex Hospital. June was called and she came with me in the ambulance to the hospital. I was in bed at the hospital when I said to June that my side feels funny. She checked and called the head nurse. The nurse called the Doctor. He came in, made a few checks, gave me oxygen and off I went to the operating room. I was in the intensive care unit for ten days.

My right leg was in a full body cast and my left side was 100% paralysed. I had a stroke, due to a blood clot in my neck. I had lost my knee cap on the right side when it went through the dash. The left side of my face was paralysed and my left eye would not close. When I slept my right eye closed and my left eye stayed open. When someone came in, I would see them and say something. The nurses would put an eye cover on my left eye at night. It was a bit scary. After about three weeks it cleared up.

## Believer in seat belts has close call

Re: Still on crutches, alderman advocates seat belts, by Lasha Morningstar (*Journal*, April 23).

As I sit in my office, I have a reminder on the wall of a serious accident I had in 1976. Had it not been for the use of a seat belt, that accident could have been considerably more serious than it was.

My reminder is a plaque presented to me by the president of the Alberta Safety Council making me a member of the "Saved by the Belt Club."

I am a firm believer in the use of seat belts. All my family uses them when driving their vehicles or riding in mine.

As an owner of a major trucking company in Alberta, I have decals on three sides of all our trailers which say: "Buckle up, seat belts work."

The sooner this government passes a law stating everyone must wear seat belts the better. People in accidents who don't wear seat belts should not be covered by Alberta Health Care.

If our premier were really truly concerned about the welfare of Albertans he would pass a mandatory seat belt law.

Anything *The Journal* can do to help convince people to use their seat belts is a credit to the people of Alberta.

V.A. Mohr
Edmonton

When I got to my room they started giving me physio twice a day. June worked with my left side when she was there. Very slowly movement came back but feeling never fully returned. I was transferred to the Charles Campsell Hospital and was not fully discharged for a total of three months. Dr Huk, my dentist from Fort Saskatchewan came in to the hospital and did some work on my teeth until I could get out. The last two weeks I was able to go home on weekends. I continued to take physio treatments for the next five months. It took a while to get all my teeth repaired as some were broken from hitting the steering wheel. It was while I was at Dr Huks office that he found a lump in my mouth. He decided to send me to a dental specialist to have it checked out. The dentist froze my mouth and would you believe the power went off in the office building, they only had emergency power. By the time the power came back on I needed to be refroze. After the second freezing it was okay to cut open the lump in my mouth. Would you believe there was the top half of the missing tooth.

## VLR Enjoys Success

VLR was doing pretty good and each year we would take all nine kids skiing in the mountains during spring break. My accident happened a couple of weeks prior to us going to the mountains. June and I decided to send our kids with Larry and Roger as I was out of intensive care.

We all looked forward to this annual skiing trip. There were fifteen of us. Those six teenage boys could sure pack away the food after a full days skiing. We always stayed at the best hotels - The Banff Springs Hotel, The Jasper Park Lodge, Chateau Lake Louise, and the Fairmount Hot Springs Lodge. All locations had swimming pools and didn't come cheap. But it was fun. VLR paid for everything, the seven hotel rooms, all the meals plus all the lift tickets. It was the highlight of the year for all fifteen of us.

Dan & Julie and Family Came from Gordondale to Company Party

Eating well at the company picnic at the Mohr Farm

My Dad throwing a Ringer at the Company Picnic at the farm.

Bert Chisholm and Dad Albert Mohr receiving the horseshoe trophy at our company picnic

*Company Picnic*

Rose
Bill
Bernice
Val

Carol

Company party
on the farm

# My Hospital Stay

When I came out of intensive care I was placed in a four bed room with my bed close to the door. I had lots of visitors in the hospital and at times I had to ask them to leave as I would get too tired. I lost thirty-five pounds during my stay in the hospital. I must tell you a few stories while I was in the hospital. This one time the young orderly tried to lift me and ended up dropping me on the floor. That generated some excitement and I had to be checked over by the Doctors. Another time he was giving me heck for no reason and I told him to get out or I would throw something at him. He made some smart remarks and I reached over with my right hand and threw a glass of water at him. I missed him but I hit the door and the glass and water went flying into the hall. Our room was outside the nursing station. It didn't take long for the hospital administrators to show up. He was transferred to another floor much to the delight of everyone in our room.

Another time when June was there two nurses came in to do something not sure what but they were trying to move me. That was during the days when nurses still wore uniforms. The one nurse said, "Val you can help, try pushing with your hand". The one nurse was kneeling on the bed trying to lift me. I was trying to push with my left hand that had very little feeling. My hand was under her uniform pushing on her panties. I had no feeling and couldn't see it. June and the one nurse saw it and the other nurse just got red in the face. June told me after what I had done.

While I was in the hospital I finally found a lawyer to handle my case. June and I would go to his office in a down town office building. I was in a wheel chair so we would call DATS (Disabled Adult Transportation System). They were very good; on time and most helpful. June and Larry ran VLR for those three months. When I got home I slowly started running the company. During my stay in the hospital I had lots of company it seemed like every day someone would come. The best was when June and the three kids would come up.

One day Ernie and Isabel Mohr came to see me and brought a container of cabbage rolls. I felt like I had died and went to Heaven. The meals at the Royal Alex kept you alive but not much more.

My first day at the Glenrose, when they brought me my dinner I was asked what kind of pie I wanted. I had to ask her twice as I didn't believe what I heard. It did take a while to regain the thirty-five pounds that I lost. Now after all these years I would again like to lose those extra pounds but by some other means.

I had a bedroom set up as an office so operated VLR from the house. I didn't drive for a long time and finally took lessons from the AMA to get my confidence back. The company was growing and finally we hired Lil Armstrong to come to the farm to help with the books which was a great help.

# VLR Continues to Grow

The company was growing and the need was there for more space. A 40 X 80 foot bay in a four bay condo became available in the W4 industrial park across the river just off highway 825, so we bought it. This gave us a place to park our trailers and do a little maintenance. We were taking our trailers to a trailer shop in Edmonton for some work. The tire companies did   our tire work

# Bad News Again

June was doing some part time nursing and one day she came home saying she had hurt her back lifting a person. She went on WCB and started going to various doctors. We even made two trips to a specialist in Lloydminister. Lil convinced me we should move our office to our new building, which we did. She then started working full time. June's condition was   not getting any better. In a matter of months, it was determined that she had cancer. The future was not good and we were told it would be a matter of time.

Doug and Ann Frey had just got married and the four of us went to Hawaii for a short holiday. June had just finished chemo so had to stay out of the sun for a few days. One day June and I went deep sea fishing with two others. A large storm had gone through the day prior and as a result many of the boats did not go out.  We found out later that if a boat goes out and goes beyond the corral reef they do not have to refund your money; otherwise they have to refund your money.

We should never have gone out. Our captain said the coast guard did not say we could not go out so we went. The water was so rough that three of us got sick; June was the only one to make it through. It turned out she was the only one on our boat that caught a fish and the only one all day on any of the boats to catch a fish. She caught a 48 pound mahi mahi. When we got in I had the captain make arrangements to have it mounted. The fish was shipped to Florida for mounting.

After returning home June's condition got worse and soon she was in and out of the Cross Cancer Hospital. I kept calling Florida to check on the fish and had to keep making payments. Then one day I got a call that the fish had been shipped and shortly after it was delivered. It came in a large wooden box, carefully packed. I wrapped the fish in a blanket and took it to the Cross. When I walked into her room carrying the fish she laid there on the bed cried "My fish, my fish." We got her up in her wheelchair and she had to tour the complete hospital and show off her fish. I took the fish home and hung it in the entrance of our house.

That Friday night she came home by ambulance for the last time, and returned to the hospital on Sunday morning. She passed away that same week. The Cross was the best hospital I have ever seen. The last two weeks I would spend the nights with her. I would eat with her and she was eating very little at this time. In the morning I would rush home and check on the three kids and then go into the office for a couple of hours then back to the hospital. I made my lunch for work at the hospital. The children knew what was happening and took it the best as they could. I was so proud of all of them.

June passed away on August 11, 1980 and her funeral was held in our church on August 14 with burial in the church cemetery. June had wanted to donate her organs but the Doctors said no as she simply had too much cancer in her body. Prior to her passing she picked out all the hymns for her funeral. She also helped to decide how she wanted her funeral done.

One other thing she said to me was "Val you are a people person please don't stay single after I'm gone for both your sake and the children."

The church was full with flowers from the staff customers and many suppliers. The different organizations that I belonged to were represented. It took a fair length of time before we settled for my injuries and then we settled out of court. All hospital costs also had to be paid by his insurance plus loss of wages etc. We were happy we lived in Alberta as we had no medical bills for any of her treatments.

## Nearly a Second Accident

It was in the spring of 1981 when I took Darrell, Rhonda, Barry, and their cousin Sherri to Banff to go skiing for a few days. The four were going down hill skiing. I would go cross country skiing When we left home I had for gotten my ski poles so I had to rent some in Banff. I had driven the four kids to Lake Louise to go skiing and had told them I would be back by 4pm to pick them up. I then went back to Lake Louise to ski around the lake on the ski trails.

I had gone all the way around the right side of the lake to the end and had returned back to the Hotel. I had some hot chocolate and then took off to go around the left side of the lake. I had gone about a third of the way when I came to an area where there had been a slide down the side of the mountain which closed off the path. The people had skied out on the lake about fifty feet from shore and went around the slide. I also went out on the lake following the ski trail to go around the slide area. I had gone about halfway when I stopped for a rest. I went to stand my ski poles up on the snow and would you believe that when I pushed them down on the ice they went right through the ice. There was little to no ice under me. I pulled them up and there were two round holes full of water. I broke out in a cold sweat. How do I get out of here alive? The first thought was if I go through the ice no one will ever find me. The water was freezing cold. The kids would be all left at the ski hill.

I was standing on very little ice. Slowly I started to turn around to head back. I moved painlessly slow as not to cause any movement or shaking on the ice. What seemed like for ever I got turned around to head back to shore. The first thought was do I go back in the same ski trail or do I move over and go on fresh snow. I could make only one decision and it had to be right as there was simply no room for error. I decided that I would use the same path that I went on the first time. I figured if it held me once it is now packed a little and maybe it would hold me a second time. I made the right choice and after about a half hour moving at a snail pace I made it to shore. I arrived at shore where the original trail was and literally dropped to the ground. I was totally exhausted.

I went back to the Chateau and reported the trail and continued up to pick up the four kids. The next day we went

23

home and when I returned the ski poles the fellow asked, "How did I get ice frozen on the poles three quarters up to the top?" I told him what happened he shook his head and said you are lucky to be here. The only thing I could think about was my children lost their mother in the fall and nearly lost me in the winter. I do believe I was the second "Man To Walk On Water".

I feel lucky to have escaped twice with my life and for that I am truly thankful.

## The Family All Had A Job

The first family member of mine to work for VLR Carriers was my wife June. This came about when I had my traffic accident. She suddenly had to learn how to do the dispatching; she caught on very fast. Then Rhonda came who helped in the office doing odd jobs. Rhonda did however prefer taking the pickup and going for parts in Edmonton. She could go in and be back faster than any one. She was not an office person but did enjoy doing the other work. Shannon also worked for a very brief time helping out in the office. She was very good at what she did but wanted to move on. She later went into the insurance business.

Darrell worked off and on for the company for a number of years when he wasn't busy farming. He helped run the business when ever I was away. I took him along a number of times when I made calls to customers in Calgary. He got along real good with many of the clients. His last trip with me was when we went to the elevators and dealers where we hauled anhydrous ammonia. He really enjoyed this and the customers enjoyed him as he could talk their farm language. It was fun to watch. Shortly after this trip around Alberta the cancer started to take control and he had to stop working for the company.

Shane also came and worked for the company for about a year. He worked in the shop. He helped with the maintenance and was very good at it. I would like to have had him stay longer however he also felt he wanted to move on.

Shauna the youngest never did work for VLR Carriers. She never ever needed a job. She had a part time job while going to High School and was always working at one or two jobs when she left school.

Darrell's love was farming however he would have been good at running the company. As a result, I did not have any family that was able to keep the company going.

Rhonda later married Dave Kehler and he worked for VLR Carriers for two years both as a company driver and as a lease operator. He was working for the company when they got married. They moved to a farm east of Edson in the Nojack area. They started with Beef cattle then later switched to Elk while still working for VLR Carriers.

The last family member who was involved in the company was my current wife Bernice. She would come with me when I would go to check plant sites out but most important she would come with me when I entertained our customers in Calgary. She soon found a few new shopping areas in Calgary to keep her busy during the day.

# Checking Plant Sites

We would from time to time get requests for rates for moving product from one location to perhaps one to six different locations. If it was a plant site, we often only received the legal location. For example, from NW 28-T54-R21-W4 to Peace Pipe at Fox Creek or Gibsons in Edmonton or Chevron at Fort Saskatchewan, or Procor at Redwater There were times the delivery destination may also be a legal address like above.

Sometimes we were told it was butane or propane and other times we were told it was mix. We knew if it was propane it weighed 5.1 pounds per gallon and if it was butane it weighed 5.8 pounds per gallon. If the product was a mix, it was all together different. They would give us the breakdown of the mix and we would have to figure what it weighed. Sometimes we would be told what it weighed. It was always important to know the weight per gallon as that is how we would determine how much we could load. Once we knew how much we could load we would set the minimum per load. Propane and butane always had the same minimum per load as their weight was constant. Mix could have a wide range depending on how much condensate, propane or butane it had. The minimum loads could also change depending if we were using five axle loads or trains. This could depend on the size of the storage the road conditions or even the bridge conditions in the area. There were times we could figure out the rates in the office and other times I would prefer to go out and check the locations.

We had times the company would want to build a plant and would want to know where the best locations would be to haul their product to. I remember one time Texaco wanted a rate on product from a location about half way between Edson and Fox Creek. This area is all hills and valleys and trees. The roads would be used by trucks hauling logs to the mills. These roads may not be too good or wide and you would have to envision what they would be like in a heavy rain or snow storm. Who was responsible for the upkeep of the roads? Also who owned the road? This may sound silly as one might assume that all roads in Alberta were owned by the province. This certainly is not the case as perhaps a lumber company may have built the road to haul logs out to their mill. The oil company may use the road and may or may not be paying something for its use, or looking after the road maintenance or sharing the cost.

We certainly did not want to give a rate and later find out no one was looking after the road in a big snow storm. In the case of the Texaco request I said to Bernice, "Do you want to go for a drive on Tuesday to check out a plant site?" She was a great co-pilot always willing to go. She would take her book or quilting and a way we would go. We often took a lunch along and then would stop for supper.

In this case we were back in the bush and couldn't find the location. We drove around and around and finally found another plant belonging to another company. I drove in and was in luck someone was there. Many little plants run by themselves with no operators on full time staff. They may simply drop in a few times a day or week depending on the plant. The province is full of these types of plants.

I asked the operator if he knew where the Texaco plant was going to be built and he replied follow me in your pick up and I will take you there. I was most thankful. When we arrived at the site I said are you sure this is the place? He

27

replied here are the stakes with the legal address matching what you have. I said you are right but this is un-real.

I clocked the mileage out to the main road with the pickup and back to where they wanted to haul it. Bernice said you're not going to haul out of there, are you? I said I'm sure not but I will give them a rate. I worked out a rate taking into consideration having to put on chains getting pulled by cats and up setting a trailer every so often. The rate was by the hour after we left the road.

It was not cheap but then I didn't want the business. I had learned it was better to price yourself out of the business then tell them you didn't want the business. I was in The Texaco traffic office talking to Roy their traffic manager when Keith their engineer came by. Keith put his head in the door and said "Where did you get that rate from for the plant I requested? It is three times higher than our best rate received. You should have driven out to the site and checked it out." I just laughed and said Bernice and I did drive out there. Go ahead and give it to who ever gave you the rate.

A number of months after I was again in the Texaco office visiting Roy when Keith came by and said "Is your rate still good?" "Why do you ask?" "The carrier we gave the hauling to has raised their rate three times and it is much higher than yours." I said let them haul it as they will continue to raise their rate until such time they can make some money at it. If they find at some point they can't make any money they will simply quit hauling. I to be honest don't want that plant at any price. I had heard that they had rolled a couple of units hauling out of there.

This was back in the days when people still smoked in their

28

offices. Roy smoked cigars and when ever I would call on him I would make sure I had a few very expensive cigars for him. He really liked that. He also liked taking off the afternoon to go play golf. We got along real good. The only problem he was a much better golfer then me. We did however enjoy the nineteen holes.

Bernice and Val went to a Mennonite Wedding at Gordondale A daughter of one of our drivers.

We had a number of plants in the Grande Prairie area of Northern Alberta which I would like to visit a least once a year. We had three lease operators working in this area all were Mennonites. This worked out good as I never had to worry about them drinking and missing work. The only problem they would not drive their truck on a Sunday. This generally did not matter however the odd time a plant would require a load loaded on a Sunday. Since the drivers all knew the operators and got along well together Dan would drive his unit over to the plant and park it at the loading rack and his wife Julie would come and get him. The operator would load his trailer on Sunday then Julie would drive him over after Sunday Midnight and he would start his shift. They did this for many years. Julie and Dan would stay over at our house if they had to come to Edmonton for anything.

These drivers would never come to any Christmas parties as there would be drinking and perhaps dancing so that was out. We would go up there and take them all out for a meal. They would enjoy that very much being with the boss and his wife. We made sure we never over dressed when ever we were with them.

Val receiving a Christmas Gift at the Christmas Party

Carol      Brenda  Bill
Christmas Party

Our Christmas Party

Darrell--->

31

Rhonda

Carol & Bill
Christmas Party

We did get invited to two weddings at Gordondale, Alberta. We did make it to only one as the other one was in the winter and the roads were too bad and we had to return home. Another time we went with the pick up to High Level in Northern Alberta about 450 miles north of Edmonton to see a customer who we hauled propane to for Canadian Propane. We left High Level and decided to travel north to Hay River in the North West Territories. It is on the mouth of the Hay River and is known as the "Hub of the North" It was founded by the Hudson Bay company in 1869. Neither one of us had ever been up here before. The population is about 4,000 people. Using water transportation, you can travel down the lake and on the MacKenzie River to the Arctic Ocean and on to Tuktoyaktuk know as the "Tuk"

We stopped on the side of the highway and walked down a trail to see an old Trappers cabin. It was not far, so we just left the windows wide open. When we got back the pickup was full of horse flies. We sure had a job getting them out. I had to drive and we opened all the windows included the back window and Bernice had to swat the fly until we got them out.

We could not believe our eyes when we drove into town. There were buildings about seven to ten stories high. Hay River is located on the South shore of Great Slave Lake. The lake is about 250 miles long. The shore was full of barges used for transporting freight up and down the lake, it was something to see. We stayed two nights and then returned home as Hay River is about 800 miles north of Edmonton.

# Hudson Bay

We were having supper one evening when my telephone rang. It was a call from Ron Cowan of Cigas Calgary. Ron was the person that gave VLR their first LPG hauling. Ron and I became good friends and from time to time would go for a few drinks after his day's work was complete. I would call ahead to set up a time and usually it was at the end of the day. It did not take me very long to realize that Ron already had had a few drinks.

Ron said, "Val I have someone here with me that you may be interested in talking to, his name is Gordon Sample from Hudson Bay Oil and Gas." I knew of Hudson Bay but had not made contact with anyone from that company. Gordon came on line and we talked for a few minutes.

In the LPG business the companies go out for tender on their hauling in February or March with new contracts to take effect April 1st. Not all plants could take effect on April first depending when the plants came on stream. Gordon explained that they had a number of plants that he was considering going out for tender on; all of which he had under contract with other truckers. I told him we would be very interested in submitting rates to him and I would be in Calgary next Monday and meet with him to get all the details of the plants. He said "I look forward to meeting with you. Oh, by the way would you be interested in sponsoring a curling team in the Fox Creek Oil Men's Bonspiel."

I could see what he was after but since I had one foot in the water I may as well have both feet wet. I said "Sure we will look after you, let's work it out on Monday when I am in Calgary. I'll be in your office about 11 am and then we can go for lunch."

I met with Gordon and got all the information on the plants he was going out for tender on. I agreed to pick up the entry fee for the bonspiel and four new sweaters plus the hotel rooms. It did not come cheap but that was how business was done in the early days of trucking  LPG in Alberta The team did not win much but did have a lot of fun.

We submitted our rates for the plants in question and were notified that we could start hauling from all of them on April 1st. It was a large contract and we were very pleased to get it. It did keep a number of units busy on a twenty-four hour basis.

As long as Gordon was with Hudson Bay we sponsored his curling venture to Fox Creek. Hudson Bay was a well run company and anyone doing business with them was paid well. Dome Petroleum was a growing oil company and was expanding very fast. They were purchasing all the little companies that they could get their hands on. It wasn't very long that the truckers and other suppliers were having to wait for ninety days for payment from Dome Petroleum. Freight is to be paid in fourteen days but they didn't care.

Some of the carriers doing business with them did not rebid on the hauling or simply raised their rates to offset the delay in payment. Domes' slow paying did not affect us until they purchased Hudson Bay Oil and Gas. It was then it became our problem. All of our truckers and lease operators were always paid on time and this became a problem. I met with their traffic fellow to see what could be done but was told that the company policy was to make everyone wait ninety days. What could I do? We needed the business but also needed to be paid on time.

I was in his office, his name has slipped my mind and that is just as well. For this story we will call him Dave for reasons you will see later. Well, Dave was a hockey fan and had season tickets to the Calgary Flames. It just so happened that VLR Carriers had season tickets for the Edmonton Oilers. Dave suggested that instead of us invoicing at the end of the month for hauling for the month we pre-invoice at the beginning of the month for the months hauling and then at the end of the month we would reconcile the months hauling. This then moved the payment up by thirty days. He then did some paper adjustments not sure how he did it and at times it is better not to ask. By the time Dave was finished we were being paid on everything in less than thirty days; the only trucker hauling for Dome that was being paid that fast.

As I mentioned Dave had season tickets for the Flames so I would make a point to visit him on a day that the Flames played. I would buy supper and off to the hockey game we would go. If he wanted to see a special game in Edmonton I would arrange for a couple of VLR tickets in Edmonton. The Oilers were in the Stanley Cup playoffs so I got a couple of extra tickets for a couple of games for him.

This one night the Oilers were playing in the playoffs so I flew to Calgary, made calls during the morning and ended up going to Dome prior to lunch. Dave bought lunch on his expense account and three of us headed to Edmonton to the hockey game. My wife met me at the game.

At that time there was a beer strike in Alberta and beer could not be purchased anywhere. It just so happened that the fellow that drove worked for a beer brewery so guess what?

36

"You're right!" The car was full of beer. After the Oiler win you should have seen the party in the parking lot around that car with the Calgary Flame Plates. It is not often that you see people from Calgary having a party in a parking lot in Edmonton celebrating an Edmonton win. They spent all weekend in Edmonton with some newfound Oiler Fans. Oiler fans will be friends to anyone as long as they have beer during a beer shortage.

We never had problems being paid by Dome thanks to Dave. Big companies were getting bigger as they were forever purchasing smaller companies. Dome was later taken over by Amoco Petroleum and our pre-invoicing stopped. This was not too bad as Amoco paid in thirty days so we were back to normal. I had made many calls to Amoco but could not get our foot in their door. When they took over Dome they got us. The plants that we were hauling for made it very plain to Amoco that they did not want to change truckers. We were very happy when we sold. At the time Amoco was our largest customer.

I was in Calgary visiting customers and one of them asked if I had heard about Dave from Dome. I said "No, why, what has happened?" Well the story goes that his house was raided by the police. Apparently there was some ticket making going on. He had left town and no one knew where he went. It was reported and the story goes even some police were involved. I have no idea if it was true mostly hear say.

As I sit back and look at the years from 1973 to 1997 when we owned VLR Carriers Ltd I can only think how we had contributed to the betterment of Alberta. Yes, we had accidents but we were putting on close to two million miles a year. Our national safety record rated very high at the time of selling both for Canada and the United States.

As the pictures show not all roads were pavement that we had to haul on. At the time of selling over 35% of the drivers had over a million accident free miles 50% had over 500,000 accident free miles and 12% had over 250,000 accident free miles. We had finished with a great crew of drivers when we sold. I was very proud of the team we had assembled at the time of selling.

## We Did Not Go Accident Free

We were hauling butane from Mitsue to Procor underground storage which was half way between Redwater and our shop. It was in the dead of winter and the temperature was so cold that long underwear was a must. We had just received a large snow dump and one of our lease operators had turned off hwy 825 to go to the unloading plant and he cut the corner too short. The snow plow had just gone and he did not leave the blade down to indicate where the ditch was and as a result when the driver turned, he though the trailer was still on the road. The back left wheels dropped in the ditch the product ran to the back of the trailer lifting up the front end and pulling the fifth wheel off the tractor. The trailer dropped on the soft snow and slid down the ditch up to the farmer's fence and came to rest under a high voltage power line.

We called a mobile crane company to come out and set it back on its wheels. The crane company slid it back and got it flipped on its wheels in the ditch. They were then going to lift it back on the road. I asked the operator how much weight the slings could lift and was informed that they were rated for over a hundred tons. Our trailer loaded did not weigh over thirty tons. They had the trailer up in the air over the road when the sling broke and the trailer came down on its nose. It received a large dent where it hit the road.

We got the trailer on its wheels and backed another tractor under it and took it the last half mile and unloaded it. The only damage the trailer got was when it was dropped. We had to take the trailer to Calgary for a M5 test and the dent had to be removed. The crane company sent me a bill however, I had sent them a letter that they will be receiving an invoice for the repairs caused by them. By the time we were finished getting the trailer repaired they owed VLR money. Needless to say we never used a crane company again.

All accidents after that with exception of one at High Level we used Cliffs towing to set our units back on the

Road to Zama Lake

road. We were hauling from ZAMA Alberta to Edmonton and I hired a lease operator to haul a load of LPG Mix to Gibson's Terminal. He rolled the trailer empty on his way up. He was going too fast and turned off the highway into a service station with out proper care. I could not even charge him a nickel as he hadn't earned any thing yet. Needless to say he got his walking papers. This trailer was set up by a towing company from High Level.

We made all our lease operators and had our company trucks all have Tac-O-Graphs in them. We made them limit their top speed to 90km. The Tac-O-Graph cards had to be turned in with their bills of lading. A Tac-O-Graph records how fast the truck is moving and what the engine is doing. It is great for information when there is an accident. This was also protection for the drivers. A day to remember was when Jon was coming home with a train (two trailers) when he went off the highway south of Slave Lake on number 2 highway.

**Transferring product on Highway no 2
The highway was closed for a while**

**It skidded on it's side on highway 16 West
We closed the highway**

The RCMP closed the highway and people were not too happy as there was no place to detour. While I was up there with Cliffs watching them set up the units, my phone rang and we had upset a unit on highway 16 west in front of the CFRN TV station. Cliffs send another crew out and Roger went on behalf of VLR. Larry our lease operator was following a car when it swerved to miss a large timber on the highway. Larry swerved and laid the trailer over on its side. It skidded on the pavement taking the paint off the trailer and causing the steel to go blue. He was carrying 34,000 litres of propane at the time. We had two of the main highways in Alberta closed at the same time.

It was an expensive day. It was not my policy to fire a driver when he had an accident. The driver would lose his safe driving record and would have an appointment with me. This often made a driver a better driver. To replace a driver does not mean his replacement will be better. Two large towing bills and one trailer requiring a M5 repairs in one day certainly kills the profit for the day. We had decided earlier that we would self-insure our trailers for physical damage and only cover liability. We could have replaced one trailer a year and it would still be less than the cost of the physical damage coverage for the trailers.

I will go on and explain about some of the many accidents we had. By reading this you will think we had nothing but accidents. That's not true, as these accidents are over some twenty years.

At one time we had over twenty trucks operating in Saskatchewan, Alberta and British Columbia plus some hauling into the USA. We did not do much hauling into the USA as it seemed every time we went there they wanted to renegotiate as they felt they were now a good customer. We could make more money staying in Canada then putting up

41

with that "BS."

We got a call one time from the Hinton RCMP advising that our truck and trailer had been rolled at the ramp off highway 16 heading south to Coal Valley. I said let me talk to the driver. They advised there is no driver around. We called Cliffs to send a unit out to set up the unit. We then sent another unit out to pump off the load, and deliver it to the destination. The driver had simply taken off and hitch hiked back to Edmonton. He had left his tack card in the truck which clearly indicated he was driving too fast. Needless to say this driver did not get a second chance.

While we were there pumping the Hinton fire department stayed on standby in case of accident but I think more so to gain some revenue for their fire Department. If the police requested it, there was nothing we could do since our driver left the accident. Most fire departments may know about fighting fires but know little about transferring propane from one trailer to another. Most RCMP knows even less about transferring propane. Some think they do. We received the invoice from the Hinton Fire Dept outlining what they had there for equipment and manpower to watch us transfer the load. I send them a cheque for the full amount and I thanked them for being there to assist us.

I remember one time we had an accident and a young RCMP was on the site watching Cliffs set up the trailer. This Mountie wanted to show off his stripes and kept telling everyone how it should be done. The Cliffs crew was getting annoyed and finally my safety supervisor went over and told the Mountie to get his butt over to the highway and direct traffic and leave the trailer recovery to the experts. This was the only time in twenty years that we ever had a problem with a police officer.

Another time we were coming through Sylvan Lake and there had been an accident and we were asked to go around it. As we were passing the accident we had to get close to

**Pumping off the pup**
**Bad roads**

the ditch. When we did the pup behind our trailer started to tip. The driver stopped and called the office. The lead trailer was holding the pup from tipping so there was no real problem. We called another unit of ours in the area and sent him over to pump off the pup. This was done and the unit went ahead a safe distance where they could pump the product back into the pup.

All the time a village employee was watching in his truck. After a while we got an invoice from the village for charges having their fire department on standby. The amount of the invoice was out of this world. It was about five times the invoice we had received from Hinton only a short time earlier. Hinton had two fire trucks there with crews. Sylvan Lake had a pick up with a driver. That is all. I sent Sylvan Lake a cheque for what I felt a pick up and driver was worth for the time he was there and told them that was more then fair. They cashed the cheque and we never heard from them again. Too many people feel that if it is a company it gives them the right to charge anything. A person said to me once the insurance company will pay for it so what's the problem.

That is part of the problem we see all too often today.

Armel was heading north to Zama for a load of mix when he met two trucks heading south on a high ravine. It was snowing and blowing and a car pulled out to pass the trucks when Armel saw it coming. He pulled over as far as he could with his right wheels up on the railing. The car hit the tractor so hard that it took both set of duals off the tractor and continued into the trailer duals. There was nothing left of that car. The driver was rushed to the High Level hospital and then flown to Edmonton. He lived but spent many months in hospital. We got in touch with his insurance company who was Wawanesa Insurance. Armil's tractor was an older Kenworth but it worked well. It was written off also.

I wrote his insurance company telling them to give us the go ahead to fix our trailer and that we would be charging for the loss of the tractor. Down time charges would be assessed up to the date that settlement was agreed upon. I told them what it was costing them per day for each the tractor and the trailer. I got a call asking if I would meet with their claims people from Toronto in their St Albert office. I said set the date and I will be there.

The first thing they wanted to know was where did I learn to do up claims like that. If you ever want to change jobs they would be interested in offering me a job. I left no stone unturned. The cost per day was broken down to the penny. The cost per day for licence plates and every expense I could think of was included. Overhead and management costs were included at 150% of actual costs.

I learned this from my Sherritt Claims that I had made.

There were two claims one for our trailer and one for Armels tractor. They made an interesting remark that they never pay a claim as presented. They must show that they got it reduced. "I said" I wish I knew that ahead of time. We both had a good laugh.

Little did they know I was well aware of this practice and had built in a good surplus to cover this. We agreed to drop a few days off each unit. They had two cheques cut while we were having coffee.

I met with Armel in a couple of days over lunch and asked what he would be happy with. He gave me a number and when I handed him his cheque his eyes just about popped out. He could not believe it. This was one of those few accidents that we made money on. It took the insurance company three months to get off their butts and for that they paid dearly. This doesn't happen too often. You do however stand a chance if you are in the right when you have an accident.

Another time we sent a driver down to a plant down by Three Hills for a load of NGL. We had been to this plant many times both with this driver and with others. Prior to our driver going to the plant he stopped at the bank and got some cash which he had in his lunch pail. When you load NGL mix or propane you always have two hoses hooked up a product hose and a vapour hose. The vapour returns the vapours from your trailer back to their storage tank. While we were loading another trucking company came in to load crude next to us. This driver did not hook his vapour hose up to their tank and instead vented off the vapours. The vapours blew towards the plant and soon were ignited by the heat exchangers. The fire followed the vapours back to his

45

trailer and also ours.

It wasn't too long before both sets of tires were on fire on both units. Our trailer got so hot that the pressure relief valves on the top of the trailer popped and flames were coming out the top of our trailer. When the trailer pressure dropped the valves shut. This happened a number of times. When the flames hit the heat exchanger the plant alarms went off and the plant shut down. Both drivers ran as fast as they could and were standing on the road when the operator arrived. He called a fire department and they responded and got the fire out. Both tractors were completely lost and also the other trailer. Our trailer had tires on and was completely black.

We sent another unit down to pump off our trailer and a set of wheels to move the trailer. We sent our trailer to Calgary for a M5 and check over plus new wiring and a paint job. The trailer was not hurt but it sure did look bad. Our trailer was due for its M5 inspection in about six months so it wasn't too bad.

I did up a claim for our loss and sent it to both the oil company and the other trucking company. Both would not pay us for our loss which was no

Into the ditch while being towed

fault of ours. This was the only time I needed help from our lawyer. He wrote them each a letter telling them they had two weeks to settle or they would be in court. We got a letter by return from the oil company advising that they were issuing a cheque. They then went after the other trucking company who was to blame. I'm sure they went after down time and loss of production for their plant. Our claim included such items as the money our driver lost that he put in his lunch pail, his clothes and whatever I could think of. Our lawyer said you sure don't miss much. I simply said I try not to miss anything. Our driver was driving a company truck which we leased from Pac Lease. When I leased our tractors we had the leases include all physical damage. The tractor was written off and we didn't even have a deductible to pay.

The trailer ended up with a new M5 inspection all new tires and wheels plus all new wiring and a new paint job. It was like a new trailer when we got it back.

Getting pulled out.

You sure don't want to have too many accidents at once as it can reduce your fleet. When you are running a large fleet you want to stagger your M5s so you don't have too many down at one time. It also spreads out the cost over a longer period of time.

Another time we were hauling for Texaco from a plant down by Gull Lake. It was on a call our bases. We only went when they called. Their plant was nearly full when they called

On it's side

and it had been raining hard for a few days. We questioned the road but they said they had a D8 cat on stand by. It would scrape the road for us and pull us out if necessary. While pulling us out our loaded trailer slid over the bank and rolled down the bank into a bunch of trees.

Not much of a Highway

A call went out to Cliffs again for a set up. The cat had to go down the ravine and clear all the trees in order for Cliffs to get in. It was a real mess working in the mud. We had to string about eighty feet of hoses so we could pump off the trailer. Cliffs then had to haul our tractor back to Edmonton and we took the trailer to Calgary for it's M5. It took a while but Texaco did finally pay for everything.

**Back on its wheels**

Whenever the company travelled a million miles without an accident we would give all the drivers something. We kept a running total for each driver. It didn't matter if they were company drivers or lease operators. All were treated equal. The drivers knew we were getting close to a million miles and there was talk in the lunch room about when it would happen.

I had already ordered gifts for all the drivers. One morning I got up early and drove to Calgary for a meeting with a customer. I then made calls for the rest of the day and returned home that evening. After a good supper prepared by Bernice I went to bed. About one AM I got a call from the RCMP advising me we had a roll over in the ditch on highway 16 just east of Elk Island Park. I got up and drove out there. I called Cliffs prior to going. When I got there the driver was sitting in the police car. It was a simple roll over and the trailer was empty which always makes it easier. The driver had just returned from three days off. The roads were dry and it was a clear night with the moon out.

I asked what happened and he said that a deer ran across the road and he swerved to miss it. The drivers are taught to never swerve for deer, dogs or anything small. If they are going into a ditch do not try to pull out drive straight in unless the ditch is such that you could get hurt. It is much easier to get a unit out if it is on its wheels. The tire marks were such that he didn't swerve. As far as I was concerned the driver fell asleep. When I pointed out the evidence he finally admitted he may have dozed off.

I was so mad I just about left him there to walk back. Our million safe driving awards were cut short by a day. That driver never drove for us again. Sometimes I will give them a second or even a third chance. In this case it was game over. I had gotten up early and drove all day and had meetings then had this. It was too much.

We were in an anhydrous ammonia season at which time we would hire extra lease operators to help us out. We would train the drivers giving them a full safety course and make some trips with them until both them and us felt safe that they could handle the product.

We had hired a driver from Tofield to pull a five axle trailer during ammonia season. Our driver was taking a load to Provost when he decided to spend the night at home in Tofield. Since he lived just out of town he decked the trailer on the street in town and went home with his tractor. He did not have room where he lived to turn the trailer around. He did not put any blocking under the trailer legs and instead just set the trailer on the street. I got a call during the night from the RCMP that we had a trailer on a front lawn in Tofield. I always took the number and would call them back as sometimes someone wants to play tricks. They gave me the trailer number and I looked up who was pulling the trailer and called the driver. It was his and he had just parked it there so he could have supper and get a night's sleep. He intended to be gone early in the morning. I called Cliffs and had them come to Tofield to set up the trailer. I had to call Sherritt as the load came from there and they would want their emergency response team to go out.

**Lifting an Anhydrous Ammonia Trailer in Tofield.**

We were already transferring the load when Cliffs arrived. The Sherritt team wanted the load transferred however Cliffs had set many of our trailers up while fully loaded. They simply put air bags under the trailer and would lift it up while they had a sling around the tank. While we were setting up the trailer a women walked by on her way to work in the morning. She asked me what we were doing.

I said, "Just having a training exercise." She remarked good to train people for that they don't have accidents. I agreed. Our driver saw her but she didn't see him. He remarked that she worked at the local newspaper. Had she known what had happened we would have made the front page.

At one of our safety meetings I handed out throw away cameras to all the drivers. The idea was that if they were involved in an accident of any kind that they were to take lots of pictures then turn the camera into me. I would get the pictures developed and they could possibility be used to protect both the drivers and the company.

It was shortly after I had given out the cameras that we had send two trucks with single trailers to take loads of propane to a Native community way north of Fort McMurray in the bush. Trucks could only get in there in the winter when the roads were frozen. Our two trucks were following each other a fair distance apart due to the blowing snow when all of a sudden a car came around the corner at an excessive speed and ran into the back end of our trailer.

No one was hurt but the car had considerable damage. Our driver called the RCMP on the truck phone to advise them what happened. They were told to exchange driver and insurance information and come in to their office and fill out an accident report. Since no one was hurt they would not come out to check it out.

While the driver was exchanging the information the other driver took all kinds of pictures. The pictures later showed that our unit was on the right side of the road when contact was made. Their vehicle was behind us. They had indicated that we were well over the center of the road.

Our driver filled out a report at the RCMP post and told the officer that our Fort Saskatchewan office would be in contact with them soon after

A Winter Road

he returned to Fort Saskatchewan. The pictures proved that it was not our fault. We forwarded the pictures to the RCMP and they were charged for following to close and whatever else they could be charged for. We issued a claim to their insurance for damages and down time. It was paid reasonably fast. Our driver did not lose his safe driving record and that accident paid for all our cameras that I had purchased.

One time I flew to High Level and met our driver Frenchie and went with him to Fort Vermilion in the truck. We were taking a load of

Heading down to cross the mighty Peace River

propane in on the river road. We had to cross the ice bridge on the Peace River. The speed limit was five miles per hour on the ice. If you travelled faster, you would push the water out the other side when you got to the bank. The ice bends as you drive across the river. The town had sufficient storage to last it for the summer.

Hope the ice will hold the unit.

After unloading we continued back to High Level and continued north to Zama Lake. We arrived at the camp in time for supper which was a very good meal. Frenchie loaded then slept in the truck. I slept in the camp and in the morning flew back to Edmonton with the company jet which transports men to Edmonton and Calgary. I certainly did not want to travel all day in the truck. It was a very interesting couple of days.

Val flew back to Edmonton in Private Jet
From Zama Lake .

# We did have Fatalities

One time Wayne was heading west to get a load of LPG mix to bring to Gibsons. He was following another truck and a third truck was behind him, not ours. Apparently a vehicle passed the back truck and when he pulled in front he went into the ditch and back on the highway. However, when he entered the highway he came under our trailer that Wayne was pulling. Our trailer went over the vehicle and spun it into the ditch. Our trailer did not upset. Both Wayne and the truck behind stopped but they could not find the vehicle. They called the RCMP and they came out immediately. The vehicle was found up side down in a ditch full of water. The driver was dead. It was reported in the paper that he had drowned.

When the autopsy was done the driver in his late years had just got his drivers licence back so went to town to celebrate at the bar. He was three times over his limit.

Another time Dave was on highway 22 and he hit a vehicle that didn't stop at the highway. The fellow was going home from a party and had too much to drink. The drivers' wife showed up shortly after the Police got there and became a bit wild. Seeing her husband who I believe was also killed. She was put in the back of the cruiser as she too had been drinking heavy. He was well over his legal limit. Neither Wayne nor Dave were charged and VLR Carriers did not consider these as accidents against their driving record.

Our third fatality accident occurred in Southern Alberta. Harold was pulling a B Train and was making a right hand turn off of the highway when a pickup tried passing him on the right side while he was turning. The pickup struck the

55

front of the tractor and rolled. There were two men in the truck. One was killed and the other was paralysed. Harold was not charged however we were sued and had to go to court. Our unit had fourteen lights flashing as he was making the turn. The pick up had lots of broken beer bottles and it was proven that both men had been drinking. The case was dropped and no charges were laid.

The forth accident I'm sure an angel was looking after the young girl. Our driver was hauling a five axle load of anhydrous ammonia from Fort Saskatchewan to Mundare. As he was driving down the highway through Lamont he saw a car pull up to the stop sign at the highway and stop. The next thing his trailer was bouncing all over. He got it stopped and he got out to check what happened.

There on the highway was a car totally destroyed. The driver checked the car expecting to find a body and the car was empty. The young girl got out and ran across the

The Girl was not Hurt after being run over in Lamont. She drove under our trailer

highway to call her dad to tell him she had an accident. When the police came it was determined the young girl had just got her driving licence the day before so got to take the car to school. Every window was covered with mud it was impossible for her to have seen the truck coming. I do believe she was charged for something. Our tack card in the tractor indicated that our driver was going well with in the

56

speed limit. The car was a total write off.

As the company grew we had regular safety meetings and often had speakers. We got along well with the local RCMP and often had them speak or show films. Other speakers were equipment suppliers such as Cummins or Cat dealers. At one time there were highway patrols that would use our shop for learning how to check brakes. The RCMP would often use our shop to train their new members on how to check brakes on a truck or trailer. They liked our shop as it had under floor heating and it was warm when they went under the trailers. Our mechanics would often help them out. The coffee pot was always on. If the Mounties decided that they would have a road side inspection I would get a call ahead of time. If it was a local inspection, we were often passed through without the inspection. They knew we kept our units in good shape. Other branches would often pass us through also.

This one time they were having a truck inspection and our truck was pulled over. The Mountie was wearing a pair of coveralls and he comes up to our driver's door and tells the driver he is not going to check him but to tell his boss that they are getting hungry crawling under all the units they had stopped.

A Safety Meeting
upstairs at VLR

Merilyn and Bernice making
Lunch for a safety meeting.

The driver comes into the office to tell me what happened. I described the fellow and the driver said "That's him." I told the office girls I would be back later. I went down to Tim Hortons and got a bunch of donuts and coffee and off I went. I went over to where they were holding their check stop and pulled into where they were stopping the trucks.

An officer came over to tell me to move along as this was a truck stop only. I said, "Tell that grumpy old guy in the coveralls that I have some coffee and donuts for him." He calls him and he comes over with a big grin on his face. "I didn't expect you but what took you so long?" We both had a good laugh. The other men there did not know who I was and we didn't say.

Another time one of our units was returning from the North when he lost his tail lights on highway no 2 just prior to turning on to highway 37. He had tried to get them working at night but no such luck. The Mountie stopped and said, "Where are you going?" and Louie said back to the shop. The Mountie said go ahead and I will follow you back with my lights flashing so no one runs into you. That is one way they get a good reputation.

I called the St Albert detachment and thanked them; they said it works both ways. Our drivers would often call the Mounties if they saw an accident or a drunken driver on the highway.

It was not uncommon for some of the drivers to stop behind a stranded car and offer help. I remember one time a women was stopped in a snow storm and couldn't get her car going. Our driver stayed parked behind her car and called her husband who was just a few miles away. The lady and her two children stayed in the warm truck till her husband arrived. She had been parked for some time and had no telephone to call for help. A number of vehicles had gone by in the dark.

Bert was working down in Southern Alberta hauling NGL Mix from some of the plants when I got a telephone call. He was so mad he could hardly talk.

I said "What is the problem?" He said I quit you can come and get the tank. I knew something must have happened as Bert was an older driver who had been driving for years and this was not like him. Finally, he calmed down to tell me he

**Bert and Lola
A fine Couple**

had been shot at with a high power gun. I said are you sure? You damn right I'm sure. The bullet came in the driver's door and passed under his legs and went out the other door. Antelope season had just opened and a stray bullet entered

his truck. He was a lucky man. We notified the police there couldn't do much.

**Bert Received a Travel TV and
a cheque from the company**

Bert didn't quit and stayed with us until he retired. We had a retirement party for Bert at our home on the acreage. The company gave Bert

60

and Lola a TV and a nice cheque. He certainly did not expect either.

**Bert Chisholms Retirement Party**

We had a new A train built in Calgary by Altank which was a new design. We had only made a few loads with it when the driver was heading north on Highway no 2 north of Red Deer. When the hitch broke the pup came unhooked and went into the ditch. The driver called and told me what had happened. I called Cliffs to go and pick it up. We transferred the load and cliffs returned it to the manufacturer for repairs. While Cliffs were setting up the trailer the RCMP had the highway blocked off.

The first unit in line was a trucker from the USA hauling a van heading north. He should have kept his mouth shut but instead he was giving the Mounties a rough time. They hauled him out of his truck and put him in the back seat. His truck was searched and they found a loaded gun inside which he had brought over the border without a permit. A fair amount of drugs were also recovered. A tow truck came and picked up his unit and took it somewhere perhaps to a police compound. A call was made to the company back in the States and I'm sure the driver spent some time in the crow bar hotel.

Having a sleep on the side of the highway
The Hitch Broke  A New Trailer.

Altank fixed the hitch and put on a different style from an Edmonton Manufacturer. They made us pay to have the work done and would not release the trailer until it was paid. The new hitch was much heavier and it too broke. Altank had us take he trailer to the company in Edmonton that made the hitch and again we had to pay prior to getting the pup back. We paid and picked up the pup and the next day the Edmonton Company went into receivership. The Sheriff

62

put a lock on the gate and everything inside was to be sold. Were we ever lucky to get it out on time!

We took our problem to our lawyer and sued Altank for all damages and loss of revenue. The case went to a three day discovery and they finally settled out of court. It had already made the newspapers. We had a chance to sell the tank which we did to Cigas. We kept the wheels and axles we were sure glad to get rid of it.

Central Alberta Adviser, Tuesday, February 25, 1997 - 5

**HIGHWAY CLOSED**

*A rolled over tanker trailer on Highway 2 northbound resulted in the RCMP closing the highway at the Gaetz Avenue entrance to Red Deer Feb. 16. Traffic was redirected onto the Delburne Highway westbound because of concerns about the tanker's hazardous waste cargo.* Glenn Werkman/Adviser

Our first A train we later sold the pup due to poor design.

Our pumps were run by a PTO shaft from the tractor. This worked good but certainly had its safety problems if not handled properly. The first driver that got hurt while unloading would have been killed had it not been for the quick thinking of another driver who came over and shut off his truck. This driver ended up in hospital for a while. This accident brought in occupational health and safety to investigate. They came up with a number of ideas which we tried. We did convert a number of trailers to hydraulic pumps but in the long run this was not too practical.

We later switched back to PTO shafts and made many changes to prevent further accidents. Every safety meeting it became a topic to touch on. We had another accident at Fox Creek where a driver was trying to grease his tractor while the PTO was running. He got his cloths torn off and required some time off. All trailers had signs on the sides warning of the danger of the PTO's turning. All drivers had to put safety chains up prior to using their PTO shafts. All shafts were later changed to shafts used on farm equipment which is a non-catching shaft. This worked well.

We did have a PTO accident out by Edson where the driver did not follow all safety procedures and had some clothes torn off. He had to go to the Edson hospital for a check out. When he returned to work  he had a meeting with me. He expected to be fired and perhaps he should have been let go. I however had other plans for him, whom I felt might work. I said here is a map that I want you to follow and do as it says and come back and tell our next safety meeting what you saw.  I want you to spend a least one hour at the location. I gave him a map which had good instructions on it but no name of the destination. When Jon got to the destination it was the Fort Saskatchewan Cemetery. Jon had to tell us of his accident how stupid it was and what he learned from his tour. It sure got the other drivers attention at the next safety meeting.

# Good Drivers are Rewarded

l to r. — Connie and Dave Coleman, Val Mohr, Bert and Lola Chisholm.

## Val Mohr Believes in Incentives

VLR Carriers Ltd. General Manager Val Mohr has over 20 drivers during peak season, and he likes to hire quality. And so he reasons that in order to keep the best people he should do what he can to make sure they're happy. For the past 11 years Val has been awarding plaques and all-expense paid vacations to his safest drivers, and as far as Val is concerned these little "perks" represent money well spent. Recipients must have completed 300,000 miles with the company, and at VLR's last company gathering two more drivers were presented with their plaques and trips to Las Vegas for themselves and their wives.

Val Mohr has been running VLR Carriers since he founded the company in 1971, and over the past 15 years VLR has expanded to the point where his drivers log over 1.5 million miles per year. The company has 38 propane and NH$_3$ tank trailers pulled by 17 tractor units, but during his peak season for NH$_3$ adds six or seven tractors to keep up with demand. With drivers permanently located in Valleyview, Grande Prairie, and Red Deer, and Westaskiwin. Val considers himself well placed to meet the needs of customers in the northern half of Alberta. "We're not large and we don't make a big splash, but we get the job done and we get it done right. We've carved out a place for ourselves in the northern half of the province, and we'll service that market the way we've done for the past 15 years. We expect to be around for a long time yet," he added.

I had decided that the magic number would be 300,000 accident free miles. The first two drivers to reach this requirement just so happened to be the first two drivers that we hired. Both drivers had come to VLR Carriers from Paul Dupras Trucking. Since different drivers on different runs may reach this total at different times I later had to design a modified system. The first drivers however were strictly on mileage safety. Dave Thomas and Noel Berube were the first winners. What we did was we gave each a trip for two to Disneyland for a week. Noel and Ursla took the trip and had a good time. Dave and Loretta decided to take the cash value.

THIS WEEK, Friday, September 29, 1995

## Local company wins praise for safety procedures

BY JAYNE L. BURYN

VLR Carriers Ltd., a Fort Saskatchewan trucking firm, and its drivers have earned some accolades for their safety practices.

The firm's earned-loss accident ratio is one of the lowest in Alberta. The ratio, explained Val Mohr,

**VLR Carriers celebrate almost 4 million accident free hours.**

President of VLR Carriers Ltd., is "what an insurance company pays out in relationship to what it gets in premiums."

Mohr recently presented safety awards to many of the company's drivers for "continuous accident-free driving".

A recipient of the Alberta Trucking Industry Safety Association Driver of the Month award for Edmonton and Northern Alberta for the month of May 1995, Dale Chubay of Edmonton was recognized for completing 300,000 accident-free miles. A three-day weekend in Victoria awaits Chubay and his wife, Ann, as an incentive reward for his performance.

Harold Wright of Okotoks completed a million accident-free miles and will be enjoying Disneyland with his wife Charlene, noted Mohr.

"Many letters of congratulations were received from some of the major oil companies of Calgary for his achievement."

Wright also won the July's Driver of the Month for Calgary and Southern Alberta distinction from the ATISA.

"Many other drivers received recognition for accident-free driving varying in years from one to fourteen," added Mohr, including Wayne Farrell and Ron Weiss of Redwater.

The company has 25 drivers. Twenty-four were recent award-winners.

VLR Carriers Ltd. hauls dangerous goods throughout Western Canada and parts of the United States for firms such as Amoco, Chevron and Petro Canada. Ninety-nine per cent of the work originates from Calgary.

We had been operating for a number of years when I decided that good, accident free drivers should be rewarded. I later felt that it had more meaning so decided not to give

67

cash value out again. The next winner was Bill Craig and we gave him a fly in fishing trip to Margaret Lake Lodge in Northern Alberta.

Welcome to Fish Camp
Bill received 300,000 safe driving trip

This trip was different as Roger and I both went along. Also took two customers and then I had some relatives who also wanted to go so in total there were ten of us. I chartered a plane and was lucky enough to have a pilot who liked to fish. We got up to the lake and were fishing shortly after lunch. We decided that we would all throw in some money and the person that got the biggest fish the first day would win the money.

Val caugh largest fish at fly in.

I'm not sure if we each put in $5 or $10 but when we quit for supper about 8PM, I had the largest lake trout. It stayed light nearly all night so some of the fellows fished till midnight as it was still light but they didn't beat me.

Norm giving lessons on fish cleaning

# 10 men flew to Margaret Lake to go fishing

Having a cool one after a good Days fishing at Margaret Lake .

We really had a lot of fun. That first night it really rained but we didn't care as next day we fished all day. The final day we only fished in the morning and then planned to fly home. We had a good farewell dinner and packed our stuff and put everything in the plane. The runway was a dirt runway and it was still very wet so the pilot said he would taxi down to the other end and take off back towards the lodge. We could all walk to the other end of the runway which we did. We walked to the other end and got in the plane and what do you think happened? The plane sank into the mud and couldn't move. The pilot sent everyone out to push the plane to get it moving, which we did.

He said he would fly across the lake to Fort Vermillion and send a small plane over to pick us up. We all headed back to the lodge in the mud. On the way back there were two large helicopters sitting by the side of the runway. I stopped in to ask them if they would fly us over to Fort Vermillion. They said sorry as they were on charter to the forest department for moving fire fighters working in the area and could not leave.

We got back to the lodge and ordered a drink. We had to wait to see if a plane would come over to pick us up. We could not even go down to the dock to fish as all of our fishing equipment was gone in the plane. In a short time a small four seater came over to pick up three of us. The pilot got out and his prop was damaged by the stones on the runway. He said the runway is too muddy and he would take only one and not return but would see what he could do.

There we sat and soon we heard a noise it was one of the large helicopters that was sitting on the side of the runway. The pilot said he got a call from the forest department to rescue us from the lodge. It cost us a $1,000.00 to have him fly us across the lake. Not sure who got the money but I bet it bought beer. We had no choice as we all had to get back to work.

My car was at the airport so when we got to the Fort to drop off Stu. I went to get out and he said don't bother I will just take my stuff and go. I stayed in the car, when we got to Josephburg to let Norm Dahl out and the same thing happened so I stayed in the car. We continued to Norm Smiths and the same thing so I stayed in the car again. When I got home I hauled my cloths in and brought my fish in which had all been frozen at the lodge. I had to show my big fish to Bernice. I unwrapped it and there it was, a large log with a minnow attached. Now I knew why they kept me in the car. Did we ever have a good laugh over that. The next day Norm gave me my fish, a real beauty.

Val presenting trip to Harold Wright for 300,000 miles accident free.

We then send Harold and Charleen to Victoria for a few days which they enjoyed.

Our next driver was Bob Craig and his wife Diane who we also sent to Victoria. Bob was having some health problems and said he was going to have to quit driving and sell his truck. Bob was working in the Olds area where he lived. Since Bob was quitting and was such a dedicated and good employee I cheated and gave him a trip prior to him making the magic 300,000 miles. I don't think it is necessary to say what his actual miles were. It was some what close. He was never told that he was short of the 300,000 miles.

Diane          Bob          Val
Bob received a trip to Victoria
for 300,000 accident free miles

Our next driver to hit 300,000 miles was Jim Saunders another very good driver. I got thinking that why send these men with their wife's when I like fishing. We took Jim to Terrace, BC for some salmon fishing. I took my Dad on this trip also. The fun was great but the fishing was not too good. Our guide did give us each a fish so everyone came home with something. We only caught one fish in the two days fishing. The fellowship is more important then what you catch. In 1987 Dave Coleman and his wife Connie and Bert Chisholm and his wife Lola enjoyed a paid vacation to a warm place.

## A Major Shock to Us

The week was drawing to a close and here it was Friday night and soon I would be heading home. The shop and office staff had already left and I was about to leave also when one of the drivers drove into the yard. I decided to wait and see who it was and talk to him prior to going home. The unit was parked and soon the driver came in to drop off his bills of ladings. My office light was still on so he came in to see me. My drivers knew that my door was always open so he came in. I had not seen Charlie (Not his real name) for some time so was glad to see him.

He was one of our younger drivers. He was married and had two small children I do believe they may have been both girls; however, I have been wrong before about these things. We talked about where he had come from and how his trip had gone. He had said how much he had appreciated the new truck we had recently given him to drive.It was a new Kenworth from Paclease. I asked how things were going at home as I had heard that they had up-graded to a newer home. He was very excited about their new home and went into detail to tell me about it. He said they were very thankful for his job and things had never been better for their family. I said to say Hello to his wife and we would see him again soon. With that he headed to his car to go home. It was only a day or two later when Carol called me to tell me Charlie had taken his life. I could not believe it after the conversation we had just had a few days earlier. Where did we go wrong or what could we have done? I will never know. The Church was full to morn a very likeable Man. "GOD BE WITH YOU CHARLIE"

## Our Tractors

If we roll the clock back to 1974 when we had that first meeting in our kitchen the plan was to purchase a trailer. As time went on it was never the intention to purchase or have any tractors. We had contacted Paul Dupras to agree to provide power to pull our trailers.

Company Tractors in Sept 1991 at our shop.

**Seven new Kenworths from Paclease Edmonton
They served us well.**

**Our tractors were all home today
Sept 1991**

This was done and worked well. We later went on our own
and hired the two lease operators to work directly for us. In
1979 we moved into our own building. We made
arrangements for Dave to look after our trailers. He sold his
tractor and came on staff full time as our trailer mechanic. It
was at this time the decision was made to own a tractor. We
felt it would give us more flexibility.

Dave was a good driver and could make the odd trip if
required. We purchased a new International from a dealer in
Camrose. We were slowly starting to get weight conscious so
the tractor was called a plain Jane so to speak. No sleeper
and no extras. Small fuel tanks one stack and what ever we
could do to keep the weight down. The intention was to use

it on the short trips.

Short trips generally earned us much more per mile however lease operators preferred the longer trips. A decision was made to later purchase a second tractor. This time we purchased a new Western Star and took delivery from the factory in Vancouver. Roger and Marilyn and Bernice and I all went out to Vancouver to get it. We took the train out and made a holiday out of it. Rented a car and spent a few days there. We picked up the tractor and all four of us came home in it. It had a sleeper so two people had to sit in the sleeper but it worked out. Roger drove all the way home and it took us a full two days but we were in no hurry.

As time went on we purchased three more tractors from drivers who wanted to get out of the trucking business. All tractors had the PTO's (Power Take Off) installed which meant they could pump from any of our trailers.

It reached a point that the five tractors were almost keeping one person busy in the shop. These tractors were forever requiring something to be done for example tire changes oil changes grease jobs repair wind shield wipers fix a noise here or there and the list went on. All tractors were different so we could not stock parts.

Each tractor as a rule had its own driver so I called the drivers in and asked them if they wanted to purchase the tractors and we would give them a job. If they wanted to pay off the tractor at any point and go to work somewhere else they were free to do so. We finally got rid of all the tractors and as a result required one less person in the shop.

I felt it was necessary to have some of our own tractors but we had to do it under a different system. We tried leasing a unit from International and also Ryder truck Rentals plus Packlease Rentals. We finally made an agreement with Packlease and ended up having all our tractors with them. All tractors were new Kenworths. Most of them had sleepers on them.We had them specked out to our requirements with PTOs on them and CBs installed.

Truckers all like a CB. Our lease had two important items in the contract. Pack Lease did all the maintenance on them including the wash jobs if we wanted them to wash them. We generally did all the wash jobs except when the unit was going in for a service then we let them do it. We would call a company called Fifth Wheel and they would come out to the shop with a little pick up and hook it behind the truck and drive in to Kenworth. They would leave it there for service. When it was finished Kenworth called Fifth Wheel and sent it back. I do believe they charged us $50.00 each way. If the unit was going to be a long time greater then a day or two they would provide us a different unit to fill in. They always had one extra unit with a PTO on stand by.

The other item which was even greater then the maintenance was insurance. All collisions insurance was included with no deductible. This was a major benefit. To do this our tractors were included in their total rental fleet in North America. If we wrote off a unit like the one that burned at Three Hills it did not cost us anything. We simply included the value of the unit in our claim and payment was made direct to Packlease. Most of the leases were for three or four years however if a unit was putting on miles too fast we would switch it to another run to slow the mileage down.

Packlease would often come to us and say we would like to

terminate the lease on unit 234 or whatever and replace it with a new one. We will give you a lighter one with better fuel economy. We always had new tractors with no maintenance or insurance. We only covered insurance for PL&PD. We had no property damage on our trailers. Property damage would have cost us between three and four thousand dollars per unit. We could have purchased one or two trailers per year for this cost. We were only required to carry five million dollars liability coverage however we carried ten million dollars coverage.

Both my car and truck were registered under VLR Carriers and had the same insurance. Not many private vehicles on the highway have this kind of coverage. We were not required cargo insurance on propane or LPG Mix.

We self-insured ourselves for everything else. We never had a cargo claim on any of our loads. The only cargo claim we ever had was when a friend of mine asked if I could help him out delivering gas and diesel for Hughes Petroleum in their trailer. Different trucking companies often worked for each other. We sent over our driver for training and would you believe he dumped gas into a diesel tank on his last day. We caught it right away before any one wanted diesel. We had the tank pumped out and taken back to the refinery for processing. Since we were pulling their trailer he said he would put it through his insurance. Cost would be minimum as no one had used any diesel.

I bought the supper for four of us at a nice place after the clean-up was complete. There certainly were no hard feelings.

We had a couple of plants in Southern Alberta that we required a tractor for. We made arrangements with Manites to pull a trailer for us to haul for us and look after the plants. Things were going pretty good until their dispatch slipped up and forgot to send a trailer in. The plant called our office and we rushed a unit down from the Fort. We made it just in time. We then hired our own lease operator to work down there. No more problems.

Packlease took me to Everett Washington to see one of our new tractors being built at the Kenworth factory. It was most interesting. We also went to a major league baseball game at the King dome. We saw Seattle Mariners and Toronto Jays play.

Another time they flew me up to their private lodge to go salmon fishing in Northern British Columbia. The fish were all cleaned frozen and packed for us when we flew home. The third time Bernice and I were flown out to Vancouver where we were picked up by the President of Packlease and taken down to the waterfront. We boarded their private yacht. Two other couples were there plus the president and his wife. We sailed north for four days up the coast of British Columbia. We would stop along the way and lower a small boat and go exploring into little coves. One time we lowered two boats and tried our luck at fishing. The bar had over 150 different brands to choose from. One time someone ordered something they didn't have which I didn't think was possible. They called back and it was delivered by helicopter to us. It was a fun week. The other two couples were from Los Angeles and San Francisco. When we switched our tractors to Packlease it was one of the best moves we made.

Another move we made was similar to leasing our tractor was leasing drivers. We made an arrangement with a company called Transpersonal. They were supplying all the drivers to Sears Line Haul a division of Sears's stores. They would find the drivers check them out and we would train them to haul our products. We would pay them by either the hour or by the mile. Our rate would include all the extra charges such as WCB, Canada Pension, and holiday pay and so on. They would pay the drivers and worry about all the deductions and submit to where it had to go. It made our office job much easier. If we didn't like a driver we simply called them and said we don't want him any more. We did not have to deal with the Canada Labour Board.

We treated these drivers as if they were our own similar to an adopted child. They attended all our safety meetings, company picnics and Christmas parties. They were part of the family.

I must say when I introduced this idea it did not go over very good with some of the other drivers. My safety man was not too happy either. I stood firm and finally they came around and saw my side of it. Some of these drivers had over a million miles accident free. If something happened, they were often the ones that got blamed before the truth came out.

# Helping out Young Boys

I had decided that we could use some help in the shop for cleaning up at the end of the day, perhaps after school. This job was for only a few hours in the evening and would be finished when the office and shop staff went home at about 4.30pm. The minimum wage in Alberta was $5.00 per hour however we paid our boys $7.00 per hour. As it was not always a full time job.

Over a period of time we had a number of boys. Some we had to keep an eye on as they tried to see how little they could get away doing. Some didn't know how to sweep the floor. We had one high school boy from Josephburg who was a real gem. We had asked him to sweep the shop the first day he was there. He simply moved everything picked up any garbage and did a great job. The place hadn't been that clean for years. He was always asking what else he could do. It wasn't very long and he was washing trailers. He was a big husky boy who wanted to learn everything he could. It wasn't very long and he knew how to hook the yard tractor up to a trailer and bring it in for washing. He was in his glory. He certainly had good training from home and I made a special point of telling his parents how pleased we were with him. He left us when school was out and went to work full time for his Dad.

One day we received a call from a high school in St. Albert asking if we could take a boy in for work experience a few days a week. We were not to pay him and the school Division looked after all compensation in the event he was to get hurt. They explained that the boy was having a difficult time in school. The first few times his parents would drive him over after dinner and then he would go home with our safety man

82

at night. Bill lived in St Albert. So it worked out good. We enjoyed the young man however we did have to keep an eye on him at all times, as we didn't want him to get hurt. There were some days he would come over when Bill started work and bring his lunch and spend the complete day with us. His mother phoned me one time to let me know what a change they found in him. All he could talk about was trucks and VLR Carriers. His time with us ended when the school term was finished.

We gave him a plaque for his time with us. I had ordered company jackets for all my drivers so ordered one for him with his name on. I took it to his school and gave it to him there. I'm sure if he could have walked on air he would have. His parents called to thank us for the nice gesture. They said he would wear it to bed if they would let him.

## Swamper for a Day

One morning I got up and said to Bernice I got an idea last night.

"What is it this time Val you are always coming up with something."

I said having been a single parent I'm sure there are single mothers in Fort Saskatchewan who have boys that could use a little help. I said "What I would like to do is give a boy a chance to go with a trucker for a day." She said what about girls? I said no this is for boys only. How would a girl go to the bathroom on the side of the road if the need arrived?

From "Truck News" Vol. 9, Issue 11  November 1989

# Kids are "swampers" for a day

Mounties from Fort Saskatchewan Alta. could be riding the range in LPG tanker trucks by now, in a new development of a program begun this summer for fatherless boys.

Val Mohr of VLR Carriers Ltd. in Fort Saskatchewan began the program, to give the kids a thrill and to give single mothers a break. VLR hauls LPG around the province with 25 tractors and about 50 trailers, and this summer Mohr offered to let fatherless teen-age boys ride for a day with VLR driver trainer Bill Craig. Kids who took the ride worked their way as swampers, helping pre-trip the truck before the run and setting blocks and checking tires when they stopped for coffee.

Mohr called the program "swamper for a day" and local mounties co-operated by driving the kids from their homes to VLR's terminal and back again. Some of the mounties got interested in the program too, Mohr said, and now the kids are back to school some of them want to come for a ride on their own time.

Mohr, a vice president of the Alberta Trucking Association, reported his program to the ATA board of directors and now the association is looking at extending it to other areas. One possibility, he says, is that scale-men and transport inspectors may be invited out for a day's ride.

The kids program continues too, Mohr says, but with school in session kids can only go when Craig has a Saturday run.□

# Truckers program for troubled youths

by Simon Blake

A Fort Saskatchewan trucking company is sponsoring a unique program to help troubled teens.

V.L.R. Carriers Ltd. is inviting children, particularly boys from single parent homes, to become a "swamper for a day."

The company plans to send one or two boys aged 10-16 out on day-long trips on company semi-trucks each week.

"Some of these boys don't have much opportunity to do things," said company owner Val Mohr. "It's not often that boys that age get to go on a 26 wheeler."

The trips give the boys exposure to the trucking industry, and Mohr hopes some of them will consider truck driving for a future career.

"It may at some point also save a boy's life if he knows how long it takes one of those rigs to stop," he added.

The first trip took place last week. Carl Banman, 12 went to Rocky Mountain House with veteran driver Bill Craig who has racked up over a million accident-free miles.

It wasn't a free ride. Craig kept Carl working throughout the trip, performing all the regular duties of a swamper, or helper.

Carl checked the oil, put blocks under the truck's wheels every time they stopped and checked tires with a hammer during several walk-around inspections.

They arrived at Rocky Mountain House natural gas plant around noon.

Carl said one of the most interesting parts of the trip occurred while the truck was being filled with 50,000 litres of natural gas liquid.

"Bill took me in and showed me the instruments and stuff at the plant."

Once both trailers were filled, the pair headed home, arriving at 6:30 p.m.

Carl, a Grade 7 student at Fort Junior High School, said he enjoyed the experience and would like to drive a truck some day.

His mother, Rena, was pleased that Carl had the opportunity. "I was very touched. It was really super."

She said that with no Uncles at Large program in the Fort, single-parent children can have a difficult life.

"There wouldn't be so many kids in trouble (if there were more programs like swamper for a day)."

Fort Saskatchewan community development co-ordinator Gail Steeves agrees. "The more experience you can give young kids the more options they have."

Fort RCMP are helping with the project by chauffeuring the boys from their homes to the VLR Carriers depot at the Sturgeon Industrial Park.

"It gives young people an opportunity to see what trucking is all about," said Const. Stewart Begg.

So far Mohr has been recruiting boys for the program primarily by word of mouth. However, he emphasizes, "Any single moms that have boys should contact us."

Const. StewartBegg, Val Mohr, Carl Banmen and driver Bill Craig gather on a rainy Tuesday morning before Bill and Carl drive to Rocky Mountain House. Carl was the first area youth to participate in the "Swamper for the Day" program.

I am sure there would be enough boys in the area to keep the program going. The first thing I had to do was contact our insurance company and get their approval in writing as we had a company policy no passengers unless pre approved.

Swamper for a day Nov 14.1991

85

I then contacted our lawyer who made up a release that had to be signed by the parent. The parent had to pay a dollar to make the contract legal. We then brought the RCMP into the program. Their job was to pick up the boy from their home and deliver him to the shop. We would then take a picture of the boy the Mountie and the driver beside the truck. We called the program Swamper for a Day.

## Letters to the editor
### *Swamper program draws praise*

**Dear Editor,**

I'd like to express my thanks to Val Mohr, Bill Craig and Constable Begg for giving my son, Carl a day he'll remember for a very long time (in the Swamper for the Day program reported in the July 26 Record).

What these men are doing for the fatherless boys in Fort Saskatchewan should show others how desperately an Uncles at Large program is needed here.

Thank you gentlemen for making my son so happy.

**Rena Banman**

The boy had the use of a hard hat with Swamper for a Day on it. He had to learn how to check the oil in the tractor and do all the pre trip inspections that the driver would do. I would notify both the shipper and receiver what we were doing for no one would get excited if they saw a young boy around the unit while we were loading or unloading propane. Our drivers were all handpicked for this job. On this trip the driver would stop for lunch and perhaps something to eat on the way back. We paid for both meals and lunches. The drivers liked it as they didn't have to pack a lunch. On the way home the boy got to call his Mom from the truck and tell her about what time he would be home. The driver then drove the boy home after they got back from their trip. This program was a great success and was written up in a number of trucking magazines.

Each year VLR Carrierrs would sponsor a couple of boys to be able to go to camp for a couple of weeks. We did this for about five years. All boys came from single Mom homes. They were able to ride horses and go boating and do all things that boys like to do.

## Disaster Strikes

It was on a Friday night on July 31, 1987 when I was getting ready to head home for the week end when I over heard Larry call his wife to tell her he was in from his trip and she could come out and pick him up. They lived in North Edmonton just off 167 Avenue. I said tell her not to bother as there is a storm coming and I will drive you home. It will only take me a half hour and the weather does not look very good. We headed into the city and the wind was really blowing. The radio was advising every one to take shelter as it was a possible tornado coming. We were not in tornado country so many did not take it too serious.

I got Larry home and was returning when the rain and wind started. It was unbelievable. I went straight home as fast as I could with the radio saying stay off the highways. Saturday I went over to the shop in W-4 Industrial Park and as usual.  I

87

walked through our two bays, and into the office. I probably spent a couple of hours prior to returning home.

Early Sunday morning I got a phone call from the RCMP advising our building was on fire. I was up and dressed and over there prior to the fire trucks arriving. Our building was a four bay condominium and we owned the middle two sections. Flames were coming out the end west bay at the back and were spreading fast along the roof. The top of the roof was metal however the insulation was made of compressed straw. The fire was going across one bay to the next and dropping down on what ever was under it.

All four bays were lost however the fire department was able to save our office and contents. Everything in the two end bays was lost. The person that was renting the west bay was in the flower import business. He would bring flowers from overseas and deliver them to the stores. His bay had a lot of paper and packing materials all over the floor and generally was in a mess.

Our two bays were very clean as they were all swept out Friday night prior to the staff going home. The end bay on the East was used for a boat repair shop. It had the usual materials in it used for that type of business

Our one bay on the west had two trailers in it. One was a convertible highboy that had the sides down and the other was a propane trailer. The other bay had about four or five tractors in it. The East bay had a couple of boats inside being worked on. By the time the fire was put out all contents in all four bays were lost.

# Fire destroys local trucking firm

by Simon Blake

An early morning fire destroyed a Fort trucking business recently.

However, VLR Carriers continue operation with leased trucks.

"We're operating as if nothing happened," says manager Val Mohr.

Firefighters were called to the fire, in the Sturgeon Industrial area across the river from Fort Saskatchewan, at 6 a.m., Sunday, Aug. 2.

Fire departments from Gibbons, Morrinville and Fort Saskatchewan fought the blaze for 2½ hours before bringing it under control.

Mohr estimates damage at $500,000. The five-bay industrial building was gutted.

The roof, supported by wood/steel composite trusses, had straw insulation which allowed the fire to jump from bay to bay, according to Gibbons fire chief Doug Harder.

Structural engineers are looking at the building, but haven't yet determined whether of not it can be repaired.

VLR Carriers have occupied three bays in the building since 1981.

Fire investigators have not determined the cause of the blaze. No one was in the building when the fire began, according to Harder.

VLR lost three tractors and two trailers in the fire. Two trucks were 1987 Kenworths, valued at $100,000 each.

They also lost about 60-80 truck tires, a yard truck and shop equipment.

Firefighters were able to salvage business records for the past two months, but previous records were lost.

Usually, said Mohr, only one or two trucks would have been in the building. However, the trucks were inside because they couldn't make scheduled deliveries to Edmonton businesses that were damaged by the tornado that hit Friday evening.

However, bad weather saved one truck. Lease operator Larry Stefaniuk was scheduled to work Sunday.

But, he said he started deliveries on Saturday because the weather was too miserable to do anything else.

Had he waited until Sunday, "My truck would have been in there too," said Stefaniuk.

Mohr said he was amazed to find diesel fuel in the tanks of burned trucks, even though the tops of the aluminum tanks were melted down to the fuel level.

The tornado in Edmonton made fire repairs difficult for Mohr.

An insurance adjuster had to be sent from Toronto as all Edmonton area adjusters were busy.

The fire came when VLR Carriers were busier than ever, according to Mohr.

However, he said he doesn't expect the disaster will hurt service.

So far Mohr has leased three trucks, and hopes to lease one more. He said the tornado made lease trucks scarce, as other businesses scramble to replace damaged trucks.

Mohr is working from a temporary office in a double garage, and says the company will rent a new shop within two weeks.

A marine dealer and a flower wholesale business, which share the building, were also severely damaged.

Truck driver Larry Stefaniuk looks at the remains of VLR Carriers' yard truck following a fire which destroyed their shop recently.

It took fire departments from Gibbons, Fort Saskatchewan and Morrinville 2½ hours to bring the blaze under control.

The five-bay industrial building in the Sturgeon Industrial Park was completely gutted.

## Only part saved in major fire

Nothing left after the fire

The results of our fire

# The Fire

*The VLR Transport building (below) southeast of Gibbons near Fort Saskatchewan was completely destroyed by fire on the weekend. There were no injuries in the fire, which was the scene of much concern when a fuel tank truck (above) was spotted. The tank did not explode, as was feared, and the blaze is now under investigation. Photos by Jack Dagley.*

Our office contents were the only thing saved. I called our insurance broker who called our Insurance Company and they jumped on it at once. They were going to get an adjuster over but with the tornado just two days prior there wasn't an adjuster in Edmonton that wasn't busy. They had to fly one in from Toronto. I picked the fellow up at the airport and we went straight to the fire site. He took some pictures and we went to eat after which time I drove him back to the airport. He said it is a total write off. I will give you a cheque now for $50,000.00 to help you get started and relocate. We will follow up later as we put together the rest of the claim.

It was now that the work started. We had to find a place for our office and then had to find a place where we could set up a shop. There were not a lot of places available in Fort Saskatchewan.

The Tornado had killed about 27 people when it hit Edmonton. We were living on the farm so I cleaned our garage and we used it. We had the telephone company come and hook up the telephone to the same number we had before. We moved our stuff over from the burned out building. The office was back running.

It was not uncommon to have a few mice running around in there while Brenda was working. Our next move was to move a couple of cats in with her to keep the mice down. This worked.

Trying to find a place to set up shop to keep the trailers was another job. There was simply nothing available in the Fort area. I finally located a building in the Fort behind the ESSO bulk station but it didn't have 220 power for a welder. The owner wouldn't spend the money to put it in and I didn't want to spend $15,000 to have the power company run posts to us from the main line. I was talking to a person I knew that worked on Maintenance at Sherritt and Earl said, "Just convert 110 to 220. I had never heard of such a thing but he gave me some written instructions on what to do. We purchased a 10 horse power electric motor and called an electrician to come and wire it as per the instructions. Both the electrician and my welder had never heard of this. We did it as the instructions said and plugged in the welder. Ken started running a welding bead as the electrician made the adjustments.

We soon got it good enough to use for welding. This then solved our welding problem. The power company sent a fellow to see if they could convince us to put the extra poles in for the 220 line power. They wanted the extra revenue. I took him in the back and he just about flipped when he saw Ken welding with a 220 power welder off a 110 line. The ten horse power motor was converting the power to 220. We used this system until we moved out in a year.

The building was not designed for what we intended so we had to build an office plus some other changes but we finally got things back in operation. We had a small back yard where we could store a couple of trailers and a small shop good enough to work on a trailer. We got by. Every one pulled together and we made due. We were back in business so now I could turn my attention on our burned out building.

The building had been a four condo building with each condo having two over-head doors at the back and a small office and washroom in the front. We had owned the middle two condos so had four doors in the back. The end two condos were both owned by banks that had foreclosed and were renting them out. The west unit was owned by the Royal Bank and The East unit was owned by the Treasury Branch. I wanted to rebuild but first there was the matter of the two bank properties.

The banks did not want to rebuild and were paid by the insurance company so I made a deal that I would clean up all the mess for a very small cost for the land. I then had a Hutterite colony come in and clean up everything for the scrap that was there. I gave them the two burned trailers to get rid of them. They must have had twenty people there and in less than a week the mess was cleaned up after they started.

We searched for a contractor and finally agreed on Flynn Bros. Construction to put up a new building. The new building was somewhat smaller. The old building had eight large doors and our new building had five large doors on the back and one on the front. The front one was used as a drive through wash bay. The west bay was a half bay just long enough to put a tractor in. We used it for tire and hose storage and had our air compressor and boiler up stairs.

The building was heated by under floor hot water heating in all the bays. We did however have to put two large over-head gas heaters in addition in the wash bay. Our problem was that if in the winter the wash bay was full of tractors full of snow and it was thirty below with a wind blowing our water lines would freeze up to the washer. The overhead heaters fixed that problem. Our washer was a Hotsey combination washer steamer. We could then steam our trailers out if we had to go in them or switch from anhydrous ammonia to propane. It worked real good and certainly had lots of pressure.

The office and lunch room and upstairs had air conditioning. The upstairs had a stove bed room and a large conference room plus a storage room. There was also a room that had the hot water tanks and furnace for the upstairs. The lunch room had toilet and shower off it for the drivers. The office had two washrooms plus two storage rooms. We were really proud of our building.

In order to make up our claim for what was lost I had both Ken and Dave each makes up a list of what they thought was lost then we all sat down and went over everything together. We did not submit it right away as we got use to our new place we kept finding something that we hadn't purchased that was still missing.

Prior to the fire I had just purchased a bunch of new hoses for the trailers these were all in storage in the shop. I had also just received a shipment of caps and gifts that would have been given away to customers. Our new bills of lading had just been delivered to the shop, a year's supply. They were still in the boxes.

We were running all radial tires on the trailers so the decision was made to take the spares off the trailers and run without spares. If we had a flat, we could always make it to a tire shop. This gave us an additional thirty tires that we could run out. It also reduced our weight on all the trailers allowing us to haul extra weight per unit. Besides these tires we had just received a bunch of recapped tires. All of the above had not been in storage for a week when the fire took everything.

Our loss came to well over million dollars. The trucks were paid under the truck policy. The fire could not have occurred at a worse time. My daughter was getting married on August the 8th on the farm and we were trying to run an office out of our yard. The yard was a real mess so Darrell was harrowing the yard to get it to dry out so the cars could get around. The day and weekend was very nice and the wedding went off without a hitch.

Things were going good and we were real busy so we had ordered some new trailers prior to the fire.

A new yard, trailer sank into the yard no base.

# An Eye in the Sky

I was sitting in my office when Carol came in with an envelope that came in the mail. She said, "What do I do with this?"

"What is it Carol?" I asked. She was holding a ticket from the Calgary Police Department for one of our units caught by camera for speeding in Calgary. Well we will have to pay it and we will charge the driver as all drivers are responsible for their own traffic tickets. Check out who the driver was and let me know and I will talk to him the next time he is in.

It wasn't very long and Carol was back in the office with a funny look on her face. I said, "What's up Carol?" She said that trailer was not in Calgary when they reported it was speeding on the Deer Foot Trail. MY eyes perked up and I said, "How do you know?"

She said that trailer was dispatched to Saskatchewan with a load of propane that day and we have a copy of a scale ticket from the Saskatchewan weigh scale about the same time as Calgary is reporting it speeding on Deerfoot trail. I said "Leave it with me and I will follow it up."

I called the Calgary Police ticket office to have the ticket cancelled and was told their cameras don't make mistakes and we were liable for the fine. I was livid and shot off a letter to the Police department explaining I will not have a driver lose a safety bonus because a police department was not doing their job right. I Said I expect a letter back by return to apologize for the error. I said we will fight the ticket and it will make newspaper coverage.

I signed the letter
Val Mohr VLR CARRIERS President
Alberta Trucking Association President

It was only a few days after I sent the letter that I got a return letter back saying they had made a mistake in reading the photo picture and the ticket was cancelled. I felt good about our success when Carol comes in with a grin on her face and I immediately knew something was up. She said, "We got another ticket from Deerfoot Trail. I don't think you can get out of this one." She handed me the photo ticket clearly showing my pick up with my VLR licence Plate.

We paid the ticket and Carol posted the ticket on the notice board much to the delight of the drivers. At least we won 50% of the tickets that week.

Speeding tickets were very rare with the company as we had an imposed 90 km speed limit with our trucks. The purpose was for both safety and to conserve fuel. Our drivers were paid by the hour and the fuel saved more than offset the extra time it would take a driver to make a trip. Having the drivers drive at 90Km saved more in fuel costs then the extra labour cost for driving slower.

# We Got Sued

We had moved into our new building and were back in operation when we received notice that the couple that were running the flower business had gone to see a lawyer and decided to sue VLR Carriers Ltd. I'm sure with everything they had in their bay didn't come to $30,000 Their lawyer convinced them that they had a good case as the fire must have started in our bay as we had a propane trailer in the bay. That had to be the cause of the fire.

He had talked to some of the volunteer fire men. They had to make their claim prior to seven years so it was in the sixth year that the claim was made. They sued us for a million dollars plus some extra charges. We turned it over to our insurance company to handle it. A court date was set to take part in the Edmonton Court House and was scheduled to last a week.

Our insurance company tried to get them to settle out of court but they were going to make big money so they would not settle. I had taken a lot of pictures after the fire was over. They showed how clean our shop was and compared to theirs. His lawyer had the fire chief from the volunteer fire department testify and he was convinced that the propane tank must have been the cause of the fire.

Our insurance company brought an expert on fires from the United States. This person had been the fire chief of the forth largest city in the United States at age 36. He now travelled the world telling about fires and going to court cases such as ours. When our lawyer called him to the stand their lawyer tried to convince the judge that he shouldn't be allowed to testify. The judge was too smart for that and allowed him to speak.

He explained how hot a tire has to get to catch fire and what would have happened if the fire had started in the propane tank which was impossible. If the tank had contained propane the pressure relief valves would have popped. This didn't happen as their caps were still on. If the trailer had blown there would not have been a building left standing.

When the case was over our firemen said there was no way the fire had started in any of our bays. Their office was completely burned ours was not. It was his job to prove that the fire did not start in VLR and not say how it started. Our insurance company offered to settle out of court but they refused a second time. They made them a good offer but their sights were set on hitting the jackpot of a million dollars. After our expert testified they had second thoughts but it was too late.

The judge ruled that VLR Carriers was not the cause of the fire and they had to pay all court charges plus their lawyer. Their lawyer may have worked on a percentage received in which case they would have gotten off easier. Our lawyer said to me after that our insurance company could have gone after them for some of their costs however he would recommend they don't do that as he said it would be like trying to get blood out of a stone. They simply did not have the money.

# Pulling Someone Else's Trailers

During my days at Sherritt I got to know the people of Western Co-op Fertilizers Ltd traffic department. I had been to their Calgary office and plant many times. We were also hauling anhydrous ammonia for them with our trailers. It was at one of these meetings that I noticed some trailers sitting in their yard. I asked them about them and was informed that they had purchased them to haul their own product. The system worked but not as good as they had envisioned. I said we would pull their trailers.

They were interested and soon I talked them into giving VLR Carriers the use of four of their trailers. Whenever we hauled for them we had to use their trailers. We could use their trailers to haul for any one else but had to pay them a mileage fee.

We pulled two of these trailers for a few years in the early 1990's

**5 Ammonia trailers ready to work in 1991
Near the Fort Bridge**

We looked after all the maintenance but they were responsible for the five year M-5 inspection costs. This arrangement worked out good for both of us. They got their product hauled as fast as we could haul it and each season they made a little extra on product we hauled for someone else. We only used their trailers for someone else if we couldn't keep up with our own. At times it was better to use their trailers then it was to use our own. Our dispatcher soon learned when to choose which trailer. This arrangement stayed in play for both us until such time that VLR Carriers was sold.

There were times that all of our trailers were busy on LPG Mix or propane and we did not have any of our units on anhydrous hauling. We would get a call for a few loads of anhydrous and we simply used their trailers. This arrangement was a win-win situation.

We were hauling propane for Canadian Propane to many of their branches. This was product that Economy Carriers was once hauling. Canadian Propane had gone out for tender and we simply out bid them in the Edmonton area. We were given the following locations to look after: Drayton Valley, Wildwood, Hinton, Camrose, Provost Vermillion, Lloydminster, Boyle, Fort McMurray, High Level, Grand Prairie, Peace River, Grand Centre and Slave Lake in Alta. In Saskatchewan we hauled to Macklin, Lumston, North Batterford and Maidstone. We did get calls to haul to Vancouver from time to time. When this happened we used only B-trains and usually were hauling with some other carriers. Large volumes were required in a short period of time. Generally, the Vancouver material would go by train but due to snow slides the trucks had to fill in. This they did and did a very good job.

We later entered into an agreement to pull two be trains belonging to Canadian Propane. Economy Carriers had been pulling these trailers. When Economy was notified that they were going to have to give those trailers to VLR Carriers our relationship between the two carriers dropped for a period of time. We got the trailers but they required some major repairs. They certainly were not looked after like we looked after ours. I called Canadian Propane and asked them to come and check out their trailers prior to them being pulled by us. They send up some one to Fort Saskatchewan to check the trailers and they were not impressed.

Economy was given the option to repair them or Canadian Propane would have them repaired. If my memory is correct they repaired one and we repaired one prior to going into our service. Our contract was something like our contract on our anhydrous trailers. They were responsible for the M-5 five year inspections and paint jobs and we looked after the everyday maintenance. They did however get a reduced rate when we used their trailers.

103

We still made good money when using their trailers. They got much improved service. We did not bid to active to branches in Southern Alberta as our terminal was in Fort Saskatchewan and it could mean a lot of dead heading the units. We concentrated on the areas where I felt we had an advantage. Economy did have a terminal in Edmonton, however, I believe we had lower over head costs so could do it a little cheaper.

# A Imperial Oil Contract

I remember one time I was invited to a tender invitation by Imperial Oil to haul from a number of their NGL Plants in Alberta. There were eight carriers there and we each received the same package and were all told the same thing. We all had to submit our tender by a certain date and the contract was set for a certain period of time. Prior to sending in my tender I visited every site. I had a good feeling what problems we may run into.

We at the time were not hauling anything for Imperial so I did want to get our foot in the door. At the present time their product was being hauled by about four different carriers. The volumes were not great but it could be a nice fill in. VLR Carriers generally hauled their mix plants different then other carriers. We would assign so many plants to a trucker and it was their responsibly to look after the plants. That way the same drivers were always going into the plant. The plant operators really liked this system. The operators and our drivers knew each others telephone numbers and it really worked good. Some of the trucking companies worked on a dispatch system and a plant could have a different driver each time.

The one thing about Imperial was they were very safety conscious. We did not mind this but we were forever going to safety meetings. They did not mention that this is something we would have to do when we all met that first time. At one of the meetings their fellow in charge of the trucking mentioned to me that VLR did not have the best rates but we did have the best safety records of all the carriers. This is what they considered most. I felt good about that and told him you get what you pay for, and he agreed.

About eighteen months later we got a letter that they were terminating our contract. We had never had one accident or problem while hauling their product and at no time did they not have a truck when it was required. I would have said we were the perfect carrier. I called the person that send me the letter and asked him what we had done wrong? I was told that management had made the decision that they should use one carrier for all their hauling and not a number of different carriers. He said they had gone to Westcan to do all their hauling. When Imperial built their fertilizer plant at Redwater, Westcan purchased the trailers to haul their anhydrous ammonia.

I'm sure Westcan was looking for a way to keep some of the units and drivers busy during the off season. It was a good selling point on their part. Every so often we would get a call from one of their plants asking us to send a truck out as they were shut in as no truck had arrived. It wasn't too long we heard that one of the trucks had an accident.

One of the times when the operator called to ask if we

105

would send out our driver to pick up a load I told him that he would have to call Imperial in Calgary and talk to a Mr. So and So. He would have to call me before I released a truck. I guess he called Calgary and gave someone a piece of his mind. I did get a call from Calgary and acted as if I knew nothing about it. I said Jim we don't have a rate on that movement with you so I would have to work one out. He said use the same rate as you were hauling for. Jim that was a contract rate and Imperial broke the contract. Jim as I told you before you get what you pay for. We will never haul for Imperial again. I am sorry to hear that Val. To this day I will buy very little gas from Imperial.

Roger and Val 15 years of operation

Merilyn  Roger

Rogers Fish at
Comox

Val's Salmon
at Comox
B.C.

# A Michelin Tire Claim

Our aim was always to do what ever we could do to make our tractors and trailers safer. The different tire companies would visit me to tell me about why their tires were the best. We would send our tires in for recapping and depending on the brand we could get three caps from a casing, WE have had some casings give us four caps.    That is a lot of miles on a tire. To achieve this, the tires have to be checked regular for tire pressure and wear.

The Michelin salesmen was out to see me and convinced me to try their low profile tires. It would lower the trailer by over an inch. You may not think this is much but on a moving load it can mean a lot. I ordered twenty-four tires to test on three trailers. The cost was over four hundred dollars per tire. This was by no means a large tire order. Our major expenses were labour, tractor rental fuel, and tires.

We installed the tires on two of our trailers and were planning to put a set on the next trailer that required tires. I got a call from one of my drivers to advise that one of the tires had a blowout. I said to head in. He came in  and when the tire had blown it took off the fender. I called Fountain Tire out to check the tire. We had purchased the tires from Fountain Tire. I was told we ran it flat so no warranty. We took pictures of the tire and the fender.

It wasn't a week later another driver called the same problem. The back tire blew took the fender off bent the bumper and we lost the fire extinguisher. I called Fountain again and called the Michelin salesman to come out. The Michelin men came out and said our drivers should be checking their tires on regular basis and not drive them when they are low. I could hardly keep my composure, we were standing behind the trailer and I said to him take a look at those tires, the tread does not keep its width around the tire. It flows back and forth. He said, "You are right something is wrong." He took the tire serial numbers down and went back to his car and made a telephone call. He came back and said those tires had a recall. They were to come back. I said "How can they go back if you don't let the purchaser know? I think you just hoped they would go some where and no one would complain and just accept it as their problem."

What happens when a Michelin tire blows Michelin had to pay plenty to repair the damage.

Oh no that is not the case.

Your tires caused the damage to both trailers and I expect to be paid for all my out of pocket expenses.

We can't pay you for you expenses as that would admit that the tires are to blame.

If the tires are not to blame prove to me what is to blame. You can come and get all these tires. I will certainly bring this up at our next trucking association meeting. Since I am the current president of the Alberta Trucking Association it will be on the agenda for our next meeting.

"I'll tell you what we will do Val. You figure out all you costs and call me. We will give you a credit towards our regular tires which you have been using prior to switching to the low profile tires.

## VLR Carriers Ltd. rolling for 20 years

Twenty years ago, Larry Laird and Roger Henry asked Val Mohr to keep their anhydrous ammonia trailer busy during the wintertime.

A partnership was formed and VLR Carriers Ltd. has been rolling ever since.

The Fort company has grown from a three-man operation to a 45-employee strong enterprise in the span of those 20 years.

With 24 trucks and 60 trailers, VLR Carriers Ltd. services western Canada and plans are in the works for expansion into the Northwest Territories and the United States.

Located in the W-4 industrial park in the County of Sturgeon, the 10,000 square foot building houses drivers, mechanics, computer operators and safety personnel.

Hauling goods such as butane, propane and LPG mixes, the company relies on cutting-edge technology and experienced staff to keep the safety standards high.

"Our commitment to safety from our drivers to our equipment exceeds government standards and always has," said owner and manager Val Mohr. "We probably have one of the best safety records in the business."

Mohr said insurance companies often recommend that other companies implement and follow VLR's high safety standards.

And being recognized as a safety leader is something Val takes great pride in.

"It says something about our company when other people want to know what we're doing right," he said.

The company offers rewards like all-expenses paid salmon fishing trips and weekends in Victoria for drivers with accident-free miles.

"We are very proud to have four drivers on staff with over a million miles each of accident free driving," Val said, adding that there is only a three per cent turnover rate among drivers.

Another thing that sets VLR Carriers Ltd. apart from other trucking companies is the fact that an estimated 96 per cent of their business comes from eight square blocks in downtown Calgary.

"Less than one per cent of our business comes from the Fort-area, but we've maintained our headquarters here because of the low cost of doing business," Val said, adding that his family has owned a farm near the Fort for over 100 years.

Another reason for maintaining VLR Carriers Ltd. in the Fort is the community-oriented environment.

As an active member of CrimeStoppers, Val knows the importance of community involvement.

That's why the company hosts a handicap student for two semesters as part of a work experience program and gives youngsters a chance to experience a truck driver's job for a day.

"We try to give back to the community as much as we can," Val said. "It makes you feel good when you can do something for someone else."

VLR Carriers Ltd. staff gather for an annual company barbecue.

As part of their community service, VLR Carriers Ltd. works closely with the

I said okay I will do that. We fixed our two trailers and added up all the costs. We got a credit for the largest amount that Michelin ever issued in Western Canada. We used up the new tire credit but did not recap the casings. We simply sent them in for casing credits. As the tires required capping we got out of Michelin tires. We found Michelin tires had a much softer casing and we could not cap them as often They would get rejected sooner. The other thing since they were softer they could not be or should not be run beside any other brand. I believe that Michelin still produces one of the best steering tires for highway tractors.

# Some Laws Should be Reviewed

When we hired a driver or lease operator they had to provide us with a copy of their driving abstract. If it had any alcohol marks on their abstract or school zone speed offence, we did not hire them. We had hired a driver and Bill our safety man went with him on a number of trips. The fellow was a good driver and caught on quick on how to handle propane so we sent him on his first solo trip to Fort McMurray. I got a call from the Fort McMurray RCMP saying our tractor and trailer was up on the meridian in town. I said "Where is the driver?" and was told he was in jail. I asked why and was told there were two outstanding warrants for his arrest. One in Alberta and one in British Columbia. Both were for not appearing in court for drunk driving charges. When the Mounties picked him up he was drunk and had been drinking vodka.

I questioned why there was nothing on his abstract I was informed that until he is proven guilty it cannot be put on his abstract. The fact that since he had skipped his court appearance has no bearing on his guilt. I complained to the attorney general department that he could have hit a school bus and killed someone. I felt something should be shown as outstanding but not charged or something. If it was on his abstract as outstanding he would not seek a driving job and may change his profession. He was released from jail and came in to pick up his cheque.

I only paid him for one way as I had to send another driver up to get the unit. He went to Alberta Labour and would you believe I lost that case too. I sure do not know where the justice is.

I would like to give you another example of some stupid

laws. This one is about log books. This is how it was then as I remember it. I have been out of the trucking industry for over sixteen years and my hair has changed color and my mind has slipped a gear or two so please forgive me if what I have indicated is a little off.

There was a ruling that if you did not travel over a 100 miles you did not require a log book. If you travelled over a 100 miles a log book was required. You could only drive so many hours per day. If you crossed a border to another province the hours permitted to drive were different.

We had a very experienced driver who had driven over two million miles accident free. A real gem of a fellow. He was hauling propane to a town just across the border in Southern Saskatchewan from Alberta when he was stopped at a road side check. He had about a half hour to go to his destination. He was ticketed. The RCMP sends a fellow over to check our files on this driver. He checked our file and found only one or two minor hour violations.

When my driver heard that we were charged he told me if the company is fined for this then he was quitting being a truck driver. I went to court in Fort Saskatchewan and the Mountie said not to worry we will talk about a plea bargain with the judge. Instead of the usual judge that usually handled this type of cases the judge was from Stony Plain. I knew by the Mounties face that he was disappointed. The judge made it very clear to me that she would not tolerate drivers who were a menace on the highway.

I paid the fine and my driver retired the next day. The industry lost a driver who had driven all his life and never had so much as a scrape. He had helped many stranded drivers and reported many drivers to the RCMP who should be removed from driving. As far as I was concerned he was a better driver then that woman was a judge. The industry lost a great driver. That night when I got home Bernice asked how my day in court went. I told her and said I think it is time to sell and get out of trucking. The injustice and all the regulations is becoming too much. I then started my search to find a buyer which took a while.

## Things went from bad to worse

We were enjoying success and had recently ordered a couple of new trailers and had purchased two used C trains to help us keep up with the volume of work we had. The bank was all in favour of loaning us the money. Our records of making our payments were always ahead of time, sometimes as much as three months. We had a bank loan for just over a million dollars and all of our customers were blue chip companies. We were always paid however sometimes the bigger the companies the slower they paid.

Our first unforeseen problem came when our building burned down. We had lots of unforeseen costs. The next problem was that the interest rates started to rise. Before long we were paying 22% interest on our loans. That is a lot of money to be paid out each month. It all had to come out of profits which did not run at 22%.

Every so often Bernice would say do you think you could maybe get a pay cheque this month. Things are getting pretty tight. I would then issue my self a small cheque to keep our house going.

We never missed a pay cheque to any of the employees and it never was late. The bank made a suggestion that we should take the building out of VLR Carriers and put it in as company by itself. VLR would then rent the building from the company. At first I was sceptical about the idea but we talked it over with our accounting firm and they said it could work. We could lower our monthly payments to the bank by a lot. This turned out to be a God send even if I didn't trust the bank.

I still don't put a lot of trust in them. I feel the banks first interest is the bank shareholders not their customers. Little did we know then that by splitting out the building it would be easier to sell the company.

We ran a really tight ship and finally the interest rates started to drop a little. The rates dropped to under 20% and I took Bernice out for supper. We hung in there and the rates dropped to the mid-teens over a period of time. We were winning but the pressure was getting to me. We had to continue to hold the line and from time to time some of the staff rebelled and in one case one of the employees took us to the Alberta Labour board. The employee had been with us for a long time and we felt we should be a little more giving. Roger and I had a meeting and had decided what we should offer. We had a couple of meetings with the Labour board representative and he had met with the employee and together they came up with a dollar amount that the employee would be happy with. It was presented to me. It was one of those cases that the employer doesn't usually win. I said if we accept what happens next. He said the employee must sign a form and the case is closed and he cannot reopen it again. We must pay the amount that was agreed on.

This was sometime ago and perhaps the situation is much different today. I had a cheque made up and gave it to the Government Rep. He presented the cheque to the employee only after the form was signed. The employee was happy he got what he had wanted and the Government employee was happy that he had completed a favourable transaction for the employee.

Roger my partner would come over from time to time and was well aware on what was going on as we had discussed it. We had decided what we felt would be fair but we were at the mercy of Labour Canada. Roger asked how I made out with Labour Canada and what we settled for. I told him and he said I don't believe it. That is less than half of what we had agreed we could pay. I said yes you are right but the employee got what he wanted and Labour Canada believes they taught us a lesson.

If I was to have offered more they would have felt that they had been cheated. This way they both won and we were also a winner. We did make sure we never got in that position again. We did however have a situation with another employee who was a good worker but had a few problems that needed correcting. I had talked to the employee a few times about it and each time logged it in their file to give me backup. I did not want to go through another Labour board issue. We were prepared to let the employee go and give a settlement better then the law said we would have to do.

The employee came into the office one day to see me with a list of demands, about ten items. That all had to be changed. On the bottom of the list it said all items must be changed with in two weeks. If they are not changed, "I QUIT."

Well that was like flying a red flag in front of a bull. I did nothing and after eight days the person came to see me to advise me I hadn't done anything and had only two days left to get the changes done otherwise she was gone. I was asked what I was going to do and when.

I said I accept your resignation and will pay you for the next two days and you can leave now. "But that is not what I wanted." I went and had a cheque made up making sure we paid the maximum that was necessary to pay. The employee took the cheque and left. I did learn a lesson from Labour Canada.

After that first encounter with Labour Canada I would call the fellow that handled the first case and say Chuck (not his real name) I am going to be in Edmonton, can I buy you lunch? He was always willing to go out. He was most helpful but did have a civil servant attitude.

## Our Equipment changes

Our equipment changed as we started to spread out into other areas. Our first trailer was a five axle highboy. It was a cheap trailer and we started hauling some sod. We then purchased a B-train highboy which gave us more capacity for hauling sod in the summer. We slowly expanded in to hauling some lumber. Since the passing of June my son Darrell took over the farming of our farm and allowed me to devote all my time to running VLR Carriers Ltd.

He started to expand and was always looking for different areas to market his grain. He made a connection to ship a load of wheat to Prince George BC with another carrier. This looked like a good possibility so we decided to purchase a trailer that we could use to haul his grain out to Prince George. We purchased a convertible hopper bottom B train Highboy. This would allow us to haul grain and feed to British Columbia and return with lumber or what ever we could find.

**Taking a load of Darrell's Wheat to the chicken farmers in Prince George, B.C. They used two loads a week.**

# A B-Train of lumber

## Our new A train Hopper Grain Trailer.

I found it interesting going after business for this new section of our fleet. I was like a boy with a new toy. The tanker business was running well and the girls in the office were doing a good job keeping these trailers busy. I found it interesting making contact with the lumber companies the saw mills farmers and feed companies. It didn't require me to wear suits and visit someone in a fancy office on the 34th floor in down town Calgary tower. At times we could do just as well with a $15,000 trailer as a $100,000 trailer. Our maintenance was a lot less. As I made contact with these new customers they soon got use to having calls for loads come from our office staff.

We hauled a load of feed to a farmer at La Crete in Northern Alberta. This was a French community. The farmer had a real French accent. I could understand him but it was difficult. I called Carol to talk to him and when she started in French I think he felt he died and went to Heaven. Whenever he called he never asked for Carol he wanted to talk to Frenchie. They got along real good. We hauled a fair bit of feed to him and back hauled lumber from mills in the north to the Edmonton area.

Our grain hauling business grew to the Prince George area. We were hauling wheat to a number of chicken farmers. Some of the chicken farmers had broilers and others had laying hens. I made contact with some of the feed mills in Edmonton and they then made contact with the chicken farmers. This gave us more loads to haul out there. Bernice and I would take a trip out to British Columbia and we would visit all these people. They certainly appreciated these personal visits.

We were asked to take a load out to a little place on this side of Terrace B.C. We made a visit out to see Tom and soon we were hauling on a regular base to Tom and delivering direct to some of his customers. We could split a B-Train and take some to each customer. They had not had this type of service before. We stopped at one sawmill on the way back to visit one of the shippers. We had been hauling on a regular base out of the mill and then suddenly it stopped and we didn't know why. Apparently another carrier came and cut the rates, which was good for the buyer. The trucking company was having lots of accidents and we had seen lumber spills on the sides of the highways. The saw mill was selling lots of lumber to the insurance companies. The drivers were all from a foreign country and had little to no experience hauling lumber in the mountains. From time to time the mill would call and ask if we could haul a load. I said sure but not for their rates. We use our rates or none.

It soon became known to the mills that we had convertible trailers and we were asked to haul scrap steel from the mills to scrap dealers in Edmonton. This was different business as we were paid for the hauling as soon as the scrap was unloaded. (The big oil companies often made you wait well beyond a month.) This was something new as we had to

120

make sure the scrap did not push the sides of the trailers out beyond the legal width allowed. It was only the BC scales that gave us the problem. We had no problems with the Alberta Scales. Alberta scales only worried about the weight they did not measure to see if we were too wide. If we were over width they would just sell us an over width permit. I have no idea how it is now.

**Hauling two loads of lumber from B.C. to Edmonton**

Darrell's farming grew and we purchased an "A train" hopper bottom unit. This gave more flexibility for hauling grain and fertilizer. We even tried hauling some flour but stopped after two loads as it would not flow out of the hoppers. Darrell was farming the Dow Chemical land both inside and outside their fence. If our trucks had to go inside the fence to load, then the drivers all had to have a Dow Chemical safety course. If we had a driver that hadn't taken the course he would pull along side the fence on the outside and Darrell would pull up to the fence with the combine and simply auger off the grain over the fence. This worked good.

A load of grain for the elevator

As the company was growing we had our accounting firm see what angles can be used to save on taxes. I can see how big companies have a lot of accountants to figure out ways to reduce their taxes. The cost of all the accountants is then an expense which is written off. We were advised to each set up a holding company then VLR would pay our holding company for our company bonus and the company would then pay us. This delayed paying income tax by a year or longer depending on when our holding companies paid us.

My company was V&J Management, Rogers was Spire Investments and Larry's was Buy Two. Larry's company name suited him. Whenever we would meet and I would suggest that I felt we should purchase another trailer Roger would say "Do we need it?" "Can we not get by"? Larry would say if we need one let's buy two. I would get my trailer. I never asked the partners about purchasing the highboys or grain trailers. They had made enough on bonus that they had faith in my judgement.

**Roger Val and ⬛️ Larry 10 years in business**

**Bernice & Val**

**Happy Birthday Val**

**Can you Type?---->**

One time in our old building prior to the fire it was my birthday and we were all up stairs in our little lunch room having coffee in the afternoon. All of the office staff, shop staff and a number of drivers were there. They had ordered a large birthday cake

125

for me. Out of the furnace room which adjoined the lunch room came this young girl all dressed up and singing happy birthday to my Valentine. She sure did have the make up on. She of course had to sit on my knee much to the delight of all the staff. They had hired her and hid her in the furnace room when I wasn't watching. The Boss doesn't know everything. I got home with lipstick all over however my wife had been alerted ahead of time. Everyone had fun.

**Our 10th anniversary**

Sturgeon Valley Fertilizers installed an anhydrous ammonia tank in the back of our yard. This tank was to service their customers in the Fort Saskatchewan and Josephburg areas. This tank worked real well for us as we would use it to train our drivers in how to unload Anhydrous Ammonia. The tank was there for many years.

Setting up the Anhydrous tank on our lot for Sturgeon Valley Fertilizers Ltd.

We also had a tank installed underground so we could blow down our ammonia trailers prior to steaming them. This also worked very well. The third item we had installed was an underground fuel tank. This was operated by a key lock system. This worked well as a lot of our trucks would come home each night so did not have to leave with full fuel tanks when going out. If the drivers didn't run with full fuel tanks, the more products they could haul. Our lease operators also purchased fuel from us from time to time. Our price was better than they could purchase it from the pumps. We would then tender out our fuel to the companies.

We had prices from all the companies and the area sales rep from Shell was a young lady trying hard to get our business. We dickered back and forth and finally I said if you come down two cents a litre you may have a deal. She gave it some thought and finally agreed. I said how do work your air mile credit. She looked at me and said air miles is only for fuel from service stations. I said it does not show that anywhere in any of your letters or brochures to me. I want it. We got a watered down version of air miles.

Installing our fuel Tank in our yard

I told her that since she was so cooperative I would do something for her. "Oh what is that Mr. Mohr?" We will pay you every time a load is dumped into our tank. You will not have to invoice us or bill us.

"That is great," she said.

I said "We will be paying by Visa." She almost fell off her chair. "No way," she said.

Every week Shell would deliver five to seven thousand gallons of diesel to us and we would pay by Visa. That is a lot of litres of diesel. Our visa collects air miles for every dollar spent. It added up. I am sure Shell did not lose any money.

Office staff going for a ride for the day learning how it is done

Three Lease operators waiting to unload

Do you want my phone number ?

998-2876

What some people will do for attention

Hauling Propane to a Paving plant We did lots of this work.

# A Shop Accident

We were getting pretty busy in the shop and had hired a mechanic to work for us. We had a pump to repair and he was going to repair it. He was told to make sure the pump did not have any propane in it prior to taking it apart. He did not follow instructions and when he opened the pump there was an explosion and he got burned He was rushed by STARS ambulance to Edmonton where he was treated.

Burned mechanic Richard Supervich, centre, is loaded into a STARS rescue helicopter Oct. 29. Supervich was one of the first patients transported by the new Northern Alberta air ambulance.

## Explosion burns worker

### Helicopter rushes man to hospital

By Kevin Franchuk

A Fort Saskatchewan man will need skin grafts to his back after he was badly burned in an industrial explosion Oct. 29.

Richard Supervich, 52, suffered third degree burns when gas leaking from a VLR Carriers tank trailer he was working on exploded at about 3 p.m.

Supervich, a contract mechanic in his sixth month of work with the Sturgeon Industrial Park firm, was rushed to Edmonton's University Hospital by STARS air ambulance.

His wife Darlene said Thursday that Richard is in stable condition, but could face a long healing period including skin grafts. He suffered burns to about 50 per cent of his body.

"His spirits are up. He is alert, but he can't talk" because of tubes doctors put down his throat, she said. "He's quite frustrated by that."

Maintenance supervisor Bill Craig said about three to four litres of liquid petroleum gas escaped from a pump on the tank and ignited. How the accident happened is still under investigation by the company, RCMP and the provincial Occupational Heath and Safety department.

It touched off a small fire, which was quickly dowsed by Craig and company president Val Mohr.

Both men also received oxygen treatment at Fort Hospital after inhaling fumes from the chemical fire extinguishers.

The explosion caused virtually no damage to the interior of the company's shop yet mangled three large overhead doors, said Craig.

He couldn't provide a damage estimate, however.

We of course had to report the accident and it took some time for the powers to determine if we were a provincial or Federal company. It was decided that since we operated both with in the province and out side the province we were a Federal company. We then fell under Federal Regulations. The person that came out was a woman who had great pleasure in showing her authority. She said that the person should have been supervised and not left on his own. The mechanic had his journey man papers. That is why you hire a journeyman. He told us he had his journeyman ticket and was being paid that way. Another thing she told us our flare stack was too high and had to be lowered. Our shop people said she had to be kidding. They could not believe it. Every flare stack in the country is the highest spot at a company. The changes were made by the time she came back for the inspection. We were approved. After much discussion with their people it was suggested it be raised back up.


## Another Fire

One time I was in the Fort having dinner with a supplier when my phone went off. The building around the corner from us was on fire. I returned at once. The company that was renting the building collected used oil filters for disposal. They had them all outside in plastic bags on pallets. Some government employee came around and told them they had to be stored inside the building. They transferred all the pallets inside the building. In less than forty-eight hours they caught on fire due to internal combustion.

The Fire department came and put out the fire with thousands of gallons of water. To avoid the water from going into the sewer system a cat came in and dug a large hole on our property to catch the oily water. The water was then pumped into large metal tanks prior to being treated before disposal. Trucks then hauled gypsum from Exshaw to our site to be mixed with the dirt that was removed from the hole in the ground. It all had to be neutralized. It was later hauled to the county land fill site. New soil and gravel had to be hauled. This operation went on for weeks. All the time a government employee had to sit and watch the operation in a big fancy motor home.

I went out to the shop one Saturday afternoon dressed in blue jeans and cowboy boots and wandered over to where they were working with two large backhoes mixing the gypsum with the soil. The fellow came out and asked me what I was doing. I said, "Just watching the machines work. What are they doing and why?"

He went to great length to tell me about the fire and that they were treating the soil. I if it was working. "Oh yes that soil is perfectly safe now, no contamination".

"What do they do with it?"

"Oh it is hauled to the land fill."

On my way over here I heard on the radio that the land fill is almost full and they will soon have to find another one. What else can we do with it but put it in a land fill? "You said it was perfectly safe right?"

"Yes."

"Then why don't you put it back in the hole it came out of?"

"Oh we could never do that. By the way who are you?"

"I own the land you are sitting on and I'm sure glad you are not putting any of that contaminated soil in that hole." He just looked at me as I drove away. I simply don't understand how government works but I have come to belief they waste a lot of money.

# Alberta Trucking Association

When we got our feet on the ground and were operating successfully I decided that VLR Carriers should join the Alberta Trucking Association. I felt it would have some benefits to us as a company. We had only been a member for a year when Norm from Veteran Transfer called me to ask if I would leave my name stand for the board of directors of the Alberta Trucking Association. I had been attending all the meetings and had been to a number of their conventions. I had some idea how things worked. VLR was one of the smaller companies that had a membership in the Trucking Association.

## Fort Man elected president of trucking group

by Mike Rasmussen

Fort resident Val Mohr, president of VLR Carriers Ltd., was elected president of the Alberta Trucking Association for a two year period at the recent 52nd annual convention.

The convention was held during the last week of September at the Chateau Lake Louise. Mohr has been involved with the trucking association for the last 13 years and was the first vice-president and chairman of the Legislature and Procedures Committee for the last two years.

"The purpose of the association is to keep drivers aware of the changes in regulations that directly affect them," said Mohr. "The Alberta Trucking Association is made up of over 200 trucking companies in Alberta plus over 200 associate companies."

"Many of the companies are members of other trucking associations across Canada," said Mohr. All association members are interested in providing a better trucking industry for the province of Alberta and Canada.

The recent price increase in fuel costs makes operating a trucking business almost disastrous, he said.

"We (VLR Carriers)

litres of fuel a year and the cost has risen 35 to 40 per cent this year already with another seven cents per litre increase due on November 1," said Mohr. "These costs have to be passed directly to the customer."

Mohr is pleased to see the several highway Check Stops implemented by the RCMP near Fort Saskatchewan. "Those running improperly maintained rigs around the province should be pulled off the roads and repaired," said Mohr.

"Members of the association generally keep their equipment in good condition and the checks help keep all operators thinking safety," said Mohr. Mohr feels there are still approximately 200 trucking companies that do not belong to the trucking association.

The association offers a high quality health care plan to the companies and their drivers. Holding courses on the upcoming GST also helps smaller companies and drivers.

"The GST will just create a lot of paperwork as it is a direct pass on charge to the customer," said Mohr.

Two major goals for the association are an increase in the roadside rest areas and the building of a national

"Drivers can only drive so many hours per day but many times there is no place for the driver to safely pull over to stop and therefore we need more roadside rest areas."

The National Highway System would allow for uniform standards across the country. The highway load rates are different between provinces. "The weight limit for British Columbia highways is more than for Alberta highways. This means that a truck going from B.C. to Alberta would not be fully loaded through B.C. or would have to stop at the border and off-load some of the cargo before entering Alberta," said Mohr.

"Another problem is the bridges. Some bridges have a lighter load capacity than the highway and this means you cannot carry a full load, and that costs the drivers more money."

The National Highway System plan is at the third stage with the plan going ahead once the fifth stage of the study is completed.

"The plan is costly but now the government collects more in road taxes (eg. fuel) than what they spend on highways," said Mohr.

Replacing Mohr as first vice-president is Joe Bogach of Grimshaw Trucking with Gregg

as second vice-president.

Mohr was the association's representative on the Standard Council for the Canadian Trucking Association for the last two years. With his election as president,

Mohr will serve as a director for the Canadian Trucking Association for the 1991-92 term.

134

# Local heads trucking group

A local trucking company operator was recently named president of the Alberta Trucking Association.

Val Mohr, president of VLR Carriers, was elected to a two-year term at the group's annual meeting in Lake Louise.

The association is a lobby group made up of about 200 trucking companies, along with a handful of independent operators.

Mohr, a 13-year association member who has served as vice-president and on the board of directors, said one of his priorities is making truckers aware of recent changes in Alberta highway regulations.

He said it's important for operators to understand the changes in hours of service laws, dangerous goods hauling and other areas.

"They should do their homework better." Ideally, Mohr added, would be a common system of highway rules across the country.

"We need a national highway system," he explained, with amalgamated regulations governing load restrictions, hours of work, hazardous goods hauling.

Mohr, who's operated VLR Carriers for 15 years, said the industry today is extremely competitive, with "too many trucks chasing after too little freight."

He cited disputes by independent truckers in Alberta, British Columbia and Ontario during the summer, who blocked roads and organized convoys to protest low freight rates and unfair competition with American haulers.

Despite the traditional rivalry between independents and trucking companies, Mohr said the association is welcoming more independents.

He said the group offers benefits like a health care plan and a unified voice in lobbying the government.

Bernice and I went to the convention and I got elected to the board of directors. Instead of starting at the bottom I got the job as first vice president. The president resigned after a year as he changed jobs and I moved up to take his position, a job I had for over two years. This was a real learning curve. I got to do a lot of travelling across Canada and in most cases my wife would come with me. One time the presidents and general managers of the four western provinces and the presidents and general managers of the Western States had a two day meeting in San Francisco.

Our group said, "Val you pick a place for some good Chinese food tonight." I asked the fellow from San Francisco where to go. He gave me a name and I booked it for most of us. Our wives were along. We had a nice meal at a very pricey place. It was a good thing we were all on association expense accounts. When we left the first thing said where is there a place to get something to eat, we are still hungry.

Three of our fellows who were down alone hailed a cap and said find us a good Chinese place. They were taken to a place and told to go down stairs. They had more to eat and drink for a fraction of what it cost each of us. Did they laugh! Whenever we went to a convention Bernice and I would take some extra time and tour the area. We got to see all of Canada travelling from Victoria to Halifax about three times to each province. We did make two trips to Newfoundland on our own.

The trucking association was most helpful when my first wife June passed away. When my son Darrell passed away Bernice and I got cards and flowers from our many friends across Canada.

It used to be a custom that at each convention the host province would have an open bar in a hotel suite. I felt after my first year that this was not a good idea as there was always someone who could not control their drinking. My second year I had the practice changed we had food to eat, coffees but no booze. I was prepared to take the heat. Manitoba did the same thing that year. Gerry Reimer was President of the

Manitoba Trucking association. He and I got along well together. We both stuck to our guns. I simply did not feel the trucking industry needed the press coverage if someone was to have an accident caused by our hospitality room. As far as I know it has not changed back to open bars.

We enjoyed travelling across Canada going to the National finals of the truck rodeos. Most of the conventions were held at nice hotels in the various cities. The Alberta conventions were held at the Banff Springs Hotel, The Chateau Lake Louise and the Jasper Park Lodge. It was at the Jasper Park Lodge that I was presented with Trailmoble Man of the year award. It was a large picture in black and white sketched of my self by an artist from Toronto.

Val receiving the Trailmobile Award in 1992

It was at this convention that I took all my kids and two grandchildren to the convention. They got to see the presentation to me.

*Jasper Convention 1992*

Shane    Shannon  Darrell  Nicholas
Bernice    Dave    Val    Margo

Shauna
Rhonda    Tiko

Donovan

Whenever I had to go to a National Convention any where in Canada Bernice was included. Our trucking association picked up all the costs for her. Her costs were also included when I went to the National truck Rodeos. I got a pleasant surprise one day when I got a telephone call from a Keith who was working for the Provincial Government and was a member of the Northern Alberta Transportation Association. He said I was nominated by the association and had chosen me to receive the Northern Alberta Transportation Man of the year. We went to the reception which was held in the Fantasy Land Hotel at West Edmonton Mall. I received a nice plaque. It said the Following......

1998  NATIONAL
TRANSPORTATION WEEK
Transportation Person Of The Year
Presented To
VAL MOHR
In Recognition of Your Leadership
And Contribution to the Enhancement
Of the Transportation Industry

Northern Alberta
Transportation Club

Golfing at Jasper 1992

Alberta Trucking Convention

# Switching Banks

We had been dealing with the CIBC bank since we started up in 1973 and things were going fairly well, however I felt when you do an evaluation of your business everything should be put on the table. This not only includes your suppliers but should also include your customers. Many companies may not look at their customers as they will consider all customers as being good. This certainly may not be the case as some customers may demand too much for what you get in return. This may include time to service them, equipment required, speed in which they pay, risk of losing money on payments due to constant requests for adjustments for whatever reason. If a customer is keeping your equipment busy it does not mean you are making money. Your returns on investment may be considerably higher by not being so busy. A little trick I learned that if a customer wants a rate on a movement and you prefer not to do business with them bid or quote high and if they give you the business at least you will make money. Always make sure you have all the conditions listed.

At one of our trucking association meetings a Carrier from British Columbia said he goes out for tender for his banking. He said he will put in his bank tender that it is for a set period of time. He said the bank knows that if they start charging him too much they could lose his business. I liked this idea so I approached my bank with a request to lower my interest rates and also the bank charges.

It appeared to fall on dead ears and nothing was done. After talking to them I had walk in calls from the Bank of Montreal and the Royal Bank. We had good discussions and I asked them to give me a proposal which they did. I returned to my bank and told them that I required a proposal from them on what they can do to adjust what they are charging me. I wanted adjustments on what we had to put up for security and so on. Not only did I give them a request on what I wanted but I told them when I wanted it by. I felt that after all I was the customer and I should have some rights. My customers required rates by a certain date other wise they would not consider VLR Carriers. Why should a bank be different?

I was in the CIBC bank and the manager called me into his office to discuss my request. He informed me that it would not be done on time as he had one person off on maternity leave and another away on holidays. I said, "Hank I really don't care about your bank problems. Those are your problems not mine. I expect it by next Friday and I will be here then to pick it up."

I returned on Friday and he did have a proposal for me. I looked it over and held it up and showed him the comparison between what I had received from the Bank of Montreal. No Comparison. He did not see the contents only the presentation. I took it back to the office and studied it in detail side by side with the new one. The Bank of Montreal proposal was considerably better in interest rates. We made the switch and stayed with the Bank of Montreal until such time as we sold the business. The Bank of Montreal was not perfect and we had to stay on top of them as they made many errors. They were always changing our contact person and banking branch. I have always said I don't trust banks. The other thing is tell them that if they want to keep your business they have to earn it. They will change be assertive and don't back down, if you are holding the Royal Flush.

# A Date with the Bears

We were hauling NGL Mix from a plant located east of Grande Prairie to the Peace Pipe unloading facility at Fox Creek on a regular basis. If it rained the road into the plant became a real mud bog. We would have to chain up both the tractor and trailer. This was a fairly large plant and it had operators on duty around the clock. Many locations we just went in to load and would leave. The operator may be there only a few hours a day. The road was very bad due to heavy rains in the area. The company was having problems keeping truckers to haul their material. I was asked to haul their material. I said I would haul but the road had to be gravelled and all towing charges and related charges would be for their account. They agreed and so we started hauling.

They did start gravelling the road when the rains stopped. We started hauling but had to chain up. Our driver had chained up and went in and loaded at the plant as usual. He then went into the plant and had coffee with the operators prior to leaving. On his way out the roads were something else and the tractor and trailer slid off the road and tipped over. The driver had put chains on both the tractor and trailer as well as the steering axle. As the truckers say they had jewellery on everything.

This was back in the 1970's and mobile phones were not like they are today. Our tractor had a telephone that you had to call a XJ telephone control tower to get out. Telephone towers were scattered across the north and you would have to try different towers to get through. If storms were in the area you often could not get through.

Our truck was on its side and his antenna could not reach

any tower to call for help. The driver was a few miles from the plant and even further from the main highway. The driver got out and there to greet him was a mother bear and her cubs. There was no way the driver could get help or return to the plant. He had to remain in his truck which was on its side until the plant operator found him at the change of his shift. This then became another challenge to set up this unit with hungry visitors watching. I was glad our contract had a condition to get us out of the mess.

It costs a lot to set up a tractor and trailer back on their wheels. The repairs and down time is something else. We had one driver hit an elk down by Drayton Valley which caused $10,000 damage to the tractor; no upset here. Before we could get a tow truck out there to recover the truck, a pickup with some native Canadians arrived, cleaned the elk, loaded it and were gone. Another time we had a moose charge one of our trucks while he was going into Zama to load. Louie was just leaving our shop with the windows open on his tractor when a swarm of bees flew in the window of his truck. He got stung pretty bad and had to return for help. It is not always that a driver had to watch out for other drivers but had to expect the unexpected from Mother Nature.

I remember one time the office staff had dispatched a driver out with a certain trailer to haul a load. The driver came in and reported the trailer was out of service. My maintenance men could not figure out what was wrong with the trailer as it had just come out of the shop a little while ago and had not been used yet. What's wrong with the trailer? Well while I was doing my pre-trip inspection I found a problem with the springs on the back left side. Go and take a look. They went and checked only to find a robin's nest with eggs in it. It remained parked till the birds left their nest.

# Partnership Splits

In 1973 sitting around our kitchen table three men decided to purchase a trailer to haul anhydrous ammonia to a storage tank at Sturgeon Valley Fertilizers on the corner of Highway no 2 and no 37. No one envisioned how this one trailer would grow into a major trucking company in Alberta. We operated under the direction of Val Mohr with ownership by the three partners all with equal shares. In 1988 Larry Laird approached his two partners asking if they would like to purchase his shares of the company. Larry had been a partner for fourteen years. Our original contract was set up that a partner had to offer their shares to the partners first. It was decided and agreed that Val would purchase the majority of the shares which gave him the major share holder of VLR Carriers Ltd. Larry did very well during his fourteen years with the company getting back over a hundred times his investment plus all the dividends and bonus. Larry was a great partner and agreed to finance my purchase over three years which worked good for me.

I always told Roger that he paid his portion by reaching into his wallet and taking out the cash. When I made my final payment to Larry we were invited to go out for supper with Pat and Larry to a nice place to eat. After supper Larry gave me a beautiful gold ring with the letters of VLR on it in diamonds.

In 1997 I had a meeting with Roger advising him that I wanted to sell the company and retire. It was always agreed that we would keep the company going as long as I wanted to run it. The first thing we had to do was determine what the company was worth. I made a list of all our tankers' size, year and M5 due dates and send it to three different trailer

146

manufactures asking for valuations for insurance purposes. We then did a full and complete inventory of everything we owned. This was done by my staff. After the fire it was not uncommon for me to upgrade our inventory. Once all this was obtained we sat down with our accounting firm to come up with a value. We required a value before and after tax. One must be careful how you sell as you do not want to affect you customer base. Or spread rumours that you are broke or so on.

# The Search

The search for buyers started with a trip to Vancouver when I met with the owner of Pacific Inland Express. They were in the tanker business and hauled from Alberta into British Columbia. They were a bit interested but felt to make it work they would like me to stay on and run the operation. I was not interested in this proposal even though I would have my money out I was still committed to working which is what I wanted to leave behind.

The next company I talked to was Chief Transportation. They were somewhat interested as our busy propane season was opposite their busy season. This would help to keep their tractors and drivers busy in their off season. I think it had the potential of working if they really wanted to make it work. The building had some interest to them. Perhaps the thing that turned them off was we wanted full payment and they did not want to go into so much debt. We did meet twice before they walked away.

I met with the owners of Mantles Carriers both in

Edmonton and Calgary. They have terminals in both Edmonton and Calgary and a good fleet of tractors. I knew the owners from the Alberta Trucking Association. From time to time we worked together. They pulled one of our trailers in Southern Alberta hauling mix. From time to time we helped them out in the Edmonton area. With the set up they had and their experience in the fuel tanker business it would have worked. They had the maintenance facilities in both cities along with the dispatch and office requirements. We both had some of the same customers. I had no idea what kind of balance sheet they had to make it work.

I met with Gibsons a couple of times and here was a carrier with both the facilities to make it work and deep enough pockets. They were familiar with the LPG mix movement as they were also in this business. The propane business was not something new for them. They knew all our customers and the problem was our customer Amaco. They felt that since Amaco was one of our bigger accounts and they went head to head with Amaco in buying mix from drillers they could possibly loose this account. They did not want to take the chance. It would have been a good fit if we didn't do business with Amaco.

I gave Gerry Reimer a call in Manitoba and asked him if they would be interested. Gerry Reimer was president of the Manitoba Trucking Association when I was President of the Alberta Trucking Association. It would have been a good fit as we were well established in the LPG business and were next door to their facility in the W-4 Industrial Park. Gerry and I talked a number of times on how it could be made to work and he made a trip out here to see our facilities. Finally, they declined to go ahead with the purchase.

I met with the president twice of Trimac Transportation. I got to know him through the Alberta Trucking Association and also the Canadian Trucking Association. They were interested but for two things I was not prepared to give it away on the terms they were interested in. The second condition was they wanted me to move to Calgary and run their complete trucking operation. To me that would be like jumping from the pan into the fire. I wanted less work not more work. This time it was me that backed out.

I met with Tom Fredericks President of Economy Carriers. We met at his office in Calgary and also had a supper meeting in Edmonton. Economy Carriers had a large terminal in both Edmonton and Calgary and hauled what we hauled for the same customer base. In fact, when it came to LPG mix and Propane we were their biggest rival. We had about 30% of the LPG business in Alberta. They appeared to be interested in order to remove their biggest opponent in the trucking business. I did not know at the time that one of the partners was having problems and that they were trying to get funding from the Ontario Teachers Association. This was relayed to me after we finally sold.

I had gone through seven different companies and winter was coming. I said to Bernice, "Let's go south for a winter holiday and we will start our search when we return." As we were going through Aldersyde I said to Bernice I'm going to stop in and see Murray Mullens of Mullens Transport. While I was president of the Alberta Trucking Association Murray was the first vice president. I knew that he had been buying up some trucking companies, so I felt it was worth the visit. I had a talk with Murray and told him what I was interested in. He went over to a filing cabinet and opens a drawer and said there is a hundred carriers that want me to buy them. I said put me in the front. Murray gave me a telephone call about three months later and asked if we were still interested in selling. I said we were still interested in selling. He said to send him a package to look at.

I sent him a package with what he required. I got a call back saying they were interested in purchasing VLR Carriers but wanted to meet with me and visit our location. Murray came up to visit our location in the evening while no one was around. I told Murray there was only three things I wanted:

No 1 - A fair Price

No 2 - All employees be offered a job

No 3 - I only want to work for a short time, not over six months.

I received a telephone call inviting Bernice and I to have supper with him and his wife in Calgary. We accepted the invitation and had a lovely supper. He said he wanted to make sure we were still interested and if so would have his lawyer send up the papers and a deposit to our lawyer. All papers were sent to our lawyer and we got what we wanted for the company. All three conditions above were met. A meeting was held with all the staff and Murray explained that all staff would keep their job.

On December 31, 1997 my working days had come to an end. I was now retired. I had spent thirty-nine years in the Transportation industry of which twenty four years were with VLR Carriers. There were many interesting years and some challenging times. Mullins purchased the business and equipment but not the building. I rented it out for a number of years and then finally sold it to my renter.

# Stollery Hospital

I would like to just print a little information about this amazing hospital connected to the Alberta University Hospital. The information shown below was all taken from various Stollery Heroes magazines over the past number of years. The purpose of this is to inform many of our readers about how the hospital was formed how it works and some of the great work that is done there.

In 1978 the Northern Alberta Children's Hospital was established. Bob and Shirley Stollery provided a very generous donation that soon became the catalyst for a dedicated children's hospital. The new hospital opened in October 2001 and in honour of the Stollery family the name of the hospital was changed to the Stollery Children's Hospital. In order to reduce over-all costs, the facility was constructed with in the walls of the Walter C MacKenzie Health Science Centre sharing space with the University of Alberta Hospital.

A friend of mine who works at the Stollery told me that the Stollery treats the sickest of the sick children in Western Canada. This covers the area from the Ontario border west to the west tip of Vancouver Island and north as far as Canada goes. This hospital is different than other hospitals in that it does many things that make the stay more pleasant for the children who have to stay there; many for extended times that can lead into years without going home.

The hospital employs many different people with different skills. Audrey Thomas is an aboriginal social worker who uses traditional methods to help make the situation less stressful for some aboriginal families who are facing

151

something very different for the first time. Dr. Kyriadides is a pediatrician at the Stollery who also does out reach clinics in Lloydminster and Inuvik. Osiris Zelaya is the VAD program co-ordinator at the Stollery who works with patients who are waiting for heart transplants. Machines are now available for small children and even infants. Osiris is a registered nurse who switched to become a specialist in a cardiac and respiratory support technique. She said the VAT program at the Stollery is one of the five best programs in the world. The program was started in 2011 and was the first hospital in Canada to use the program.

The hospital provides teachers to help children that are in for extended times and have to miss school. Computers are available for the students use. Help is provided from the lower grades through some high school. I have received a tour through this amazing hospital and one would not get the impression that it is a hospital, the windows are painted, rooms are like a kindergarten with toys and whatever is necessary to make a child's stay more pleasant. I am sure every staff member is hand picked.

The President and CEO of the Stollery Children's Hospital Foundation is Mike House MBA, CFRE. Mike is a very special type of person who can often be found out side his office working in an art class with a child. The summer 2015 issue of Heroes has a picture of Mike taking art tips from a Stollery patient Daniel Beshuizen. This is just one of the many different events in which he gets involved.

The Stollery Children's Hospital Foundation provided $3.8 million to the women and Children's Health Research Institute for children's health research. I could go on and name many people that give so much to this great hospital.

To list all the Doctors nurses and others would fill a book by itself.

The hospital was established in 2001 and 40% of all patents come from out side the Edmonton area. The hospital has 222 beds and had 215,000 patient visits in 2014-15, 153,000 were out patient visits. The hospital had 10,300 surgeries and 48,500 emergency room visits. During the year, 6 million dollars was used for equipment and facilities, 3.1 million for resources, 1.3 million for training, and 500K for programs

Cheyanne Mattern of Calgary received a double lung and heart transplant at the same time at age four. Her little chest was kept open for five days to allow the swelling to go down and to give the organs time to do their work. She is now doing well and is riding her bike and going to school. Cheyanne received a trip to Disney World at Orlando thanks to Walmart who treated other children to the magic Kingdom.

At seven years old, Lloydminster's Dillan Reid has had four major surgeries, 25 minor surgeries, more than 2,000 in-hospital and at-home procedures, and spent 634 days at the Stollery. While Dillan knows the Stollery well and loves his doctors, he's glad his visits are less frequent now that he's in the maintenance phase of Hirschsprung's disease.

Mia Richardson of Sherwood Park at 10 months had been sick with every thing from strep throat to ear infections. Her breathing became difficult and she was rushed to the Stollery. It was determined that she had diabetic complications. It is estimated she has had 10,000 needles and more than 35,000 finger pokes so far in her life. Her school has raised over $150,000 to help fight diabetes.

Ben Woodlock age 6 had to have a kidney transplant which was detected with an ultra sound test prior to being born. He received a transplant from his Dad Patrick and is now doing well.

Macy Denham of Camrose was born at 24 weeks and is now doing well at home.

This is just a little information to help you understand something about the Stollery Hospital. When you purchased this book the profits from its sale are sent to the Stollery Hospital Foundation.

Bob Stollery started work with Poole construction in 1949 as a site engineer. His business savvy, dedication and leadership helped him become president of Poole Construction in 1969. In 1977 he led the management buy out of Poole Construction which led to employee ownership. Bob was instrumental in forming the Stollery Children's Hospital. He was a great leader and builder and a very generous community person. Bob was a director of many boards during his life and received four honorary doctorates from four post-secondary institutions. In 1993 he received the Canadian Business Leader of the year and the Paul Fellow recognition from Rotary International. He also received the Prestigious Order of Canada.

*Val Mohr*
*Author*

# Haida Gwaii Totem

The Haida Totem pole comes to the Stollery from what was once called the Queen Charlotte Islands just west of Prince Rupert. In 2010 it was officially renamed Haida Gwaii. The pole stands about three meters tall and is located in the entrance of the Stollery Hospital. About 25 percent of the Stollery children are aboriginal children. Ben Williams the Carver explained that the ashes of the Haida Children that died prematurely were mixed in with the paint used for the totem. From the top down, it contains the image of an eagle, a mother bear and her cub, a bison, and some butterflies. The totem pole is made out of beautiful BC Cedar. The beauty of cedar is not only its gentle softness but its ability to outlast most other woods due to its natural oils. At one point in history the tradition of pole carving nearly disappeared. It was the Bible-thumping missionaries that discouraged such practices. This art was almost lost for nearly a century. Around the late 1800 there was a gradual return to the practice. By 1969 the art was coming back. The first modern pole was carved by the world famous carver Bill Reid in 1978. Today the art form is gaining momentum. It is making its presence felt on a true comeback with many aspiring young carvers want to take up the trade. Once again these magnificent structures are dotting the traditional Haida Nation. We can be proud to have this beautiful totem pole in Edmonton to grace the entrance of the Stollery Children's Hospital.

**The following photographs commemorate the 2015 Grey Cup win by the Edmonton Eskimos.**

Edmonton can be proud of their two major sports teams, The Edmonton Oilers and the Edmonton Eskimos who spend many hours visiting the children in hospital.

**Material republished with the express permission of Postmedia Network Inc.**

Photo by
Ian Kuceark
Edmonton Sun

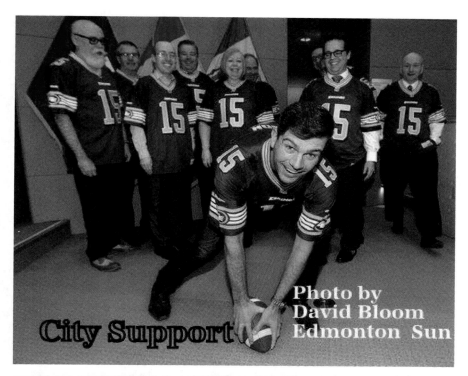

City Support

Photo by David Bloom Edmonton Sun

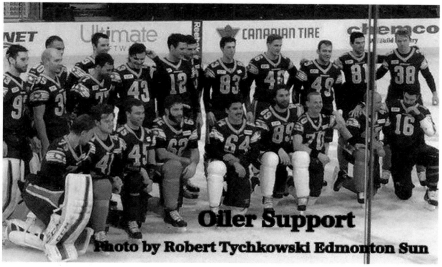

Oiler Support

Photo by Robert Tychkowski Edmonton Sun

Photo by David Bloom
Edmonton Sun

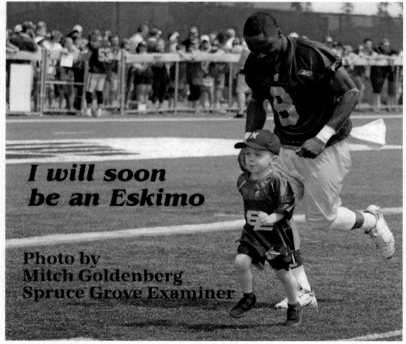

*I will soon
be an Eskimo*

Photo by
Mitch Goldenberg
Spruce Grove Examiner

A member of the
Spirit of Edmonton dancers
Performs at the Spirit of
Edmonton Party

Photo by
Brian Donogh
Winnipeg Sun

Ottawa Coach
Rick Campbell

Edmonton Coach
Chris Jones

Photo by
Al Charest
Calgary Sun

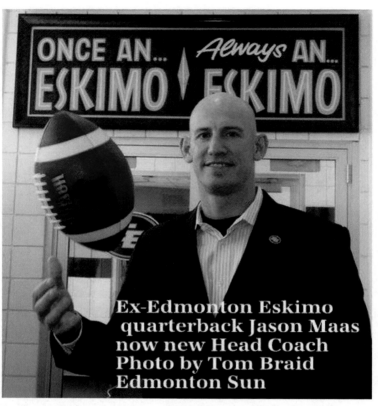

**Ex-Edmonton Eskimo quarterback Jason Maas now new Head Coach**
**Photo by Tom Braid**
**Edmonton Sun**

*Don't mess with me*

Photo by Codie McLachlan Edmonton Sun

Touchdown

Photo by Codie McLachan Edmonton Sun

Lets Party

Corey Pusey From Red Deer

Lets Party

Dave Hanni From Medicine Hat Photo by Brian Donogh Winnipeg Sun

The Best

Photo by
Ian Kucerak
Edmonton Sun

Special Delivery

Corporal
Lester Houle

Photo by
Brian Donogh
Winnipeg Sun

Corporal
Rick Sinclair

Photo by Kevin King Winnipeg Sun

Party time in Edmonton

Photo by Codie McLachlan
Edmonton Sun

GO ESKS GO

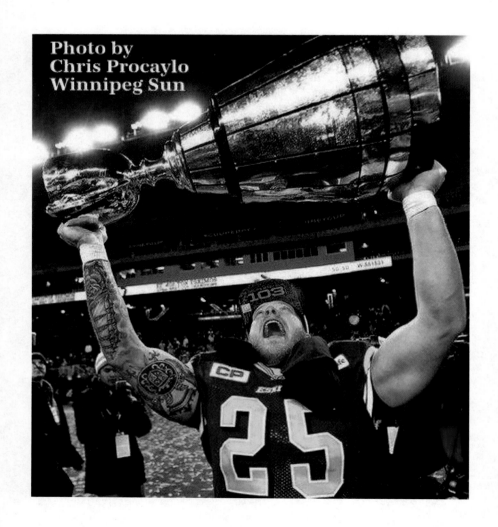

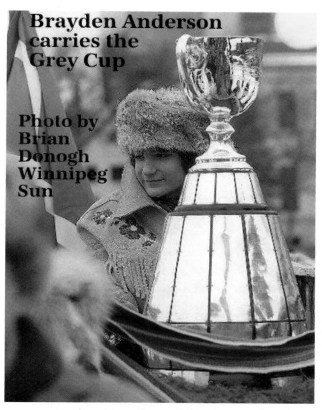

**Brayden Anderson carries the Grey Cup**

**Photo by Brian Donogh Winnipeg Sun**

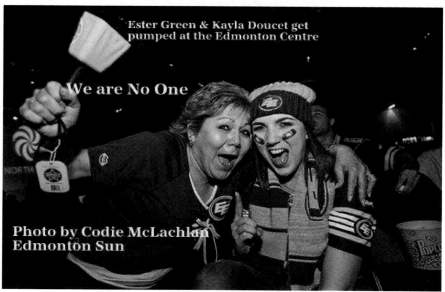

Ester Green & Kayla Doucet get pumped at the Edmonton Centre

We are No One

Photo by Codie McLachlan Edmonton Sun

Steve Klatt drinks
green and gold beer

Green

Gold

Still Standing

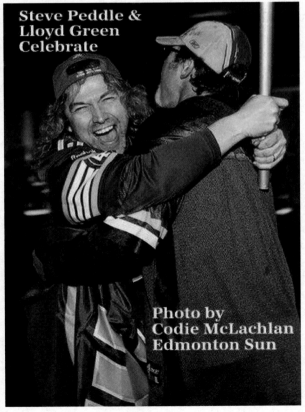

Steve Peddle &
Lloyd Green
Celebrate

Photo by
Codie McLachlan
Edmonton Sun

Kayla Doucet
doesn't hide
her Nerves

Photo by
Codie McLachlan
Edmonton Sun

Early in
the game

Our Cup
Lets Party

Photo by Cody McLachlan
Edmonton Sun

Lloyd Green,Steve Peddle,Sheldon McMillan & Ester Green celebrate the Eskimo Victory photo by Codie McLachlan Edmonton Sun

The cup returns to Edmonton in 2015

Photo by Ian Kucerak Edmonton Sun

## Book Remarks "Keep The Wheels Down"
### First and Second Edition

Knowing both your previous wife and your current wife your dedication brings a tear to my eye, just beautiful.

Retired High School Principal

I have been married to my husband for many years. It's the first book I have seen him read cover to cover.

A truck drivers wife

Val your book should have been edited, however the way it was written comes from the heart and only you could pull it off.

A Retired Judge

I have been a truck driver for many years I never noticed it wasn't edited. I can relate to some of your remarks.

A retired truck driver

The book hasn't been edited and to do so would take away what it truly is — A labour of love.

The Fort Record Oct 3/13

I enjoyed working for you and enjoyed your book more.

A Past employee

Your large print and many pictures certainly made it enjoyable to read at my age. I enjoyed the many short stories.

A Senior

I read a chapter a night and soon I was finished. It should have been longer I enjoyed it very much.

A retired plant Operator

You certainly had an interesting time in your life. Did you keep notes to remember all the details? Very interesting.

A house wife

I started reading the book and didn't stop till I was finished. Enjoyed the pictures and large print.

A retired chemist

The book explains what the company  did for young boys which trucking associations could think seriously about trying.

Western Canada Highway News  Fall  copy 2013

Val donating the profits of your book to the Stollery Children's Hospital Foundation could not be a better choice.

A retired Nurse

Your donations are a real lifeline to families like the Barths.

Stollery Children's Hospital Foundation

It was easy to read, it just flowed along. You did a good job. Thanks for writing of your stories"

A travelling friend from Ontario

The contents of the book is far more important than a few spelling and grammar errors. What you are doing for the Stollery Children's Hospital is well appreciated.

A retired  Professional

Dear Mr. Val Mohr,
My name is Emily, and I am a fourteen year old girl.

When you came into the Boyle Public Library on Thursday, to have your book put in the library I was working there. Then when I was told to place your book on the shelf, I saw the picture of your truck, I took an interest in it, and I am now reading it.

I must say, most girls my age, or even my kids my age may think that that is more of an adult book, but I must say that I love your book, and think it has been written with care and the odd mistake which is totally fine in my eyes. :)

I emailed you to tell you I think that it is a great thing you are doing, donating some of the money from selling books to the SCHF.

I have written a short (very short) story, which maybe one day I will turn into a book (after I make it longer by like 12 chapters at least) and hopefully I will do something like you are doing, donating the money to charity or something.

One thing I would like to know, is do you plan to write more books, and/or have you written more books?

Now, if you excuse me, my dad is bugging me to do my dishes, so I best be going, Thank you for viewing my email. :)
Sincerely,<br>Emily Nakonechny

My second book called "Tips Trips and Tours" and I had it printed in black and white and also had some printed with colour pictures. It covered the problems and experiences I had while travelling to seventy-five countries. I sold the black and white for $20.00 and the colour for $30.00 which barely covered the added cost. I certainly did not expect to sell many colour however they have out sold the B/W by two to one. All profit from this book was also donated to the Stollery. Both books are in a number of libraries in Alberta. Copies have been sold across Canada, many American States, and copies have gone to England, Mexico and South America.